Contents

ON the 25th of February, 2024, a young airman recorded himself approaching the Israeli embassy in Washington DC and said these words:

"I'm about to engage in an extreme act of protest. But compared to what people have been experiencing in Palestine at the hands of their colonizers, it's not extreme at all. This is what our ruling class has decided will be normal."

He then set the camera down, walked a small distance and calmly emptied accelerant over his entire body, put on his hat and lit himself on fire, uttering the words "Free Palestine" with increasing urgency as the flames took hold of his body until he physically couldn't make a sound ever again.

His name was Aaron Bushnell and this month's edition of JOHNSTONE is dedicated to his memory.

All works are written by Caitlin Johnstone and Tim Foley. The Caitlin Johnstone project is 100 percent reader-funded.

Visit caitlinjohnst.one for the original articles and their supporting links.

Coverart and original painting by Caitlin Johnstone

After ignition, he repeatedly yells "Free Palestine."

The Most American Thing That Has Ever Happened

Dateline: 24 February, 2024

A man set himself on fire outside the Israeli embassy in Washington. He said he did it in protest of the genocide in Gaza.

Independent journalist Talia Jane reports that she was able to obtain footage of the incident, which the unnamed* man apparently recorded himself. Jane reports that the man said he is "an active duty member of the U.S. Air Force" and that he "will no longer be complicit in genocide." After igniting he repeatedly yelled "Free Palestine."

According to Jane, a police officer showed up pointing a gun at the man's burning body; I guess that's just what American cops do when they aren't sure what to do. Someone who was actually trying to save the man reportedly yelled "I don't need guns, I need fire extinguishers!"

This just might be the most American thing I have ever heard of. It's more American than the fake bald eagle cries they put in Hollywood movies. It's more American than monster trucks and mass shootings. You simply cannot fit more America into a single incident than a man dying a horrifying death in protest of war crimes while a first responder screams at cops to stop pointing their guns at him and go get fire extinguishers. If you were to pick a single moment in history to sum up the essence and expression of the US empire, that would be it.

The New York Times reports that the man "was taken to a nearby hospital with life-threatening injuries and remains in critical condition." A spokesman for the US Air Force has reportedly confirmed that the man is an active duty member.

"I'm about to engage in an extreme act of protest," the man reportedly recorded himself saying before the incident. "But compared to what people have been experiencing in Palestine at the hands of their colonizers, it's not extreme at all. This is what our ruling class has decided will be normal."

The nameless protestor is correct. People in Gaza are being burned alive, are suffocating to death under collapsed buildings, are having operations and amputations without anesthesia, are starving to death, are watching their loved ones die in front of them, are experiencing suffering of a degree that very few of us here in the west can even imagine. And our ruling class is absolutely attempting to normalize this for us.

This isn't even the first self-immolation we've seen in protest of Israel's US-backed atrocities after October 7; back in December an unnamed protester with a Palestinian flag self-immolated outside the Israeli consulate building in Atlanta.

And as I reflect on this I can't help thinking, how many Israel supporters have self-immolated in protest of October 7? How many Israel supporters have self-immolated in protest of the super serious antisemitism crisis they claim is making Jews feel unsafe in their communities? Surely their grievances are just as serious and sincere as those of Palestine supporters, no?

Of course not. This has not happened and the very idea is laughable. Israel apologists insist that it is they and their favorite ethnostate who are the real victims in all this, rather than the population of Gaza who has seen tens of thousands of Palestinians annihilated while Israeli soldiers openly celebrate their mass displacement and death. But you don't see them self-immolating; you see them cheerleading for ethnic cleansing and genocide. They wouldn't do anything to cause themselves pain or inconvenience to promote their pet agenda. They wouldn't even miss brunch for it.

It's a horrific thing, burning alive. I suspect that pretty much everyone who's ever self-immolated has had serious regrets about it within the first few seconds. There's simply nothing one can do to prepare oneself for the experience of that kind of pain, or for how long it can take them to lose consciousness after it's started. At that point the only comfort they could possibly offer themselves is that it can't go on forever.

But the fact that anyone would ever take such a measure at all shows how profoundly urgent they recognize this issue to be, and how much more sincere they are about it than those on the other side.

UPDATE: The protester has died. His name was Aaron Bushnell.

●

Aaron Bushnell Burned Himself Alive To Make You Turn Your Eyes To Gaza

I watched the uncensored video of US airman Aaron Bushnell self-immolating in front of the Israeli embassy in Washington while screaming "Free Palestine". I hesitated to watch it because I knew once I put it into my mind it's there for the rest of my life, but I figured I owe him that much.

I feel like I've been picked up and shaken, which I suppose was pretty much what Bushnell was going for. Something to shake the world awake to the reality of what's happening. Something to snap us out of the brainwashed and distracted stupor of western dystopia and turn our gaze to Gaza.

The sounds stay with you more than the sights. The sound of his gentle, youthful, Michael Cera-like voice as he walked toward the embassy. The sound of the round metal container he stored the accelerant in getting louder as it rolls toward the camera. The sound of Bushnell saying "Free Palestine", then screaming it, then switching to wordless screams when the pain became too overwhelming, then forcing out one more "Free Palestine" before losing his words for good. The sound of the cop screaming at him to get on the ground over and over again. The sound of a first responder telling police to stop pointing guns at Bushnell's burning body and go get fire extinguishers.

He remained standing for an unbelievable amount of time while he was burning. I don't know where he got the strength to do it. He remained standing long after he'd stopped vocalizing.

Bushnell was taken to the hospital, where independent reporter Talia Jane reports that he has died. It was about as horrific a death as a human being can experience, and it was designed to be.

Shortly before his final act in this world, Bushnell posted the following message on Facebook:

"Many of us like to ask ourselves, 'What would I do if I was alive during slavery? Or the Jim Crow South? Or apartheid? What would I do if my country was committing genocide?'

"The answer is, you're doing it. Right now."

Aaron Bushnell has provided his own answer to this challenge. We're all providing our own right now.

I would never do what Bushnell did, and I would never recommend anyone else does either. That said, I also can't deny that his action is having its intended effect: drawing attention to the horrors that are happening in Gaza.

I know this is true because everywhere I see Aaron Bushnell being discussed online I see a massive deluge of pro-Israel trolls frantically swarming the comments in a mad rush to manipulate the narrative. They all understand how destructive it is to US and Israeli information interests for people to be seeing an international news story about a member of the US Air Force self-immolating on camera while screaming "Free Palestine", and they are doing everything they can to mitigate that damage.

As I write this, there are with absolute certainty people digging through Bushnell's history searching for dirt that can be spun as evidence that he was a bad person, that he was mentally ill, that he was steered astray by pro-Palestine activists and dissident media—whatever they can make stick. If they find something, literally anything, the smearmeisters and propagandists will run with it as far as they can.

That's what they're choosing to do at this point in history. That's what they would have done during slavery, or the Jim Crow south, or apartheid. That's what they're doing while their country commits genocide right now. People are showing what they would have done with their response to Gaza, and they're showing what they would have done with their response to the self-immolation of Aaron Bushnell.

I'm not going to link to the video here; watching it is a personal decision on which you should probably do your own legwork to make sure it's really what you want. Whether you watch it or not, it happened, just like the incineration of Gaza is happening right now. We each own our personal response to that reality. This is who we are.

•

A Profound Act Of Sincerity

One of the main reasons the self-immolation of Aaron Bushnell is having such an earthshaking impact on our society is because it's the single most profound act of sincerity that any of us have ever witnessed.

In this fraudulent civilization where everything is fake and stupid, we are not accustomed to such sincerity. We're accustomed to vapid mainstream culture manufactured in New York and Los Angeles, airheaded celebrities who never talk about anything real, self-aggrandizing Instagram activism, synthetic political factions designed to herd populist discontent into support for status quo politics, phony shitlib "I hear you, I stand with you [but I won't actually do anything]" posturing, endless propaganda and diversion from the mass media and its online equivalents which are algorithmically boosted by Silicon Valley tech plutocrats, and a mind-controlled dystopia where almost everyone is sleepwalking through life in a psyop-induced fog.

That is the sort of experience we have been conditioned to expect here in the shadow of the western empire. And then, out of nowhere, some Air Force guy comes along and does something real. Something as authentic and sincere as anything could possibly be, with the very noblest of intentions.

He live-streamed himself lighting himself on fire and burning to death in order to draw people's attention to how horrific the US-backed atrocities in Gaza actually are. Knowing full well how painful it would be. Knowing full well he'd either die or survive with horrific burns and wish he'd died. Knowing full well that once he connected the flame with the accelerant he poured onto his body, there'd be no turning back.

He didn't back down. He didn't go home and stuff his face with snacks and gossip in the group chat and see what types of mindless escapism are available on Netflix or Pornhub. He lit the flame. He even struggled to light it at first, and he still did.

There's nothing in our society that can prepare us for that kind of sincerity. That kind of selflessness. That kind of purity of intention. It stops us dead in our tracks, as if the fabric of our world has been ripped asunder. And, in a way, it has.

We're not really living in the same world we were living in before Aaron Bushnell lit himself on fire at 1 PM on February 25th. It was far too sincere an act, committed in the least sincere city on this planet. It shook things around far too much for all the pieces to fit fully back into place.

I myself am permanently changed. I find myself reapproaching the Gaza genocide with fresh eyes, renewed vigor, and invincible determination. I now write with a different kind of fire in my guts.

And looking around I can see it's much the same for others. Where previously we'd begun seeing the opposition to the incineration of Gaza beginning to lose a bit of energy due to despair and how hard it is to keep something energized for months on end, we are now seeing electrifying enthusiasm.

More importantly, this is shaking things up in mainstream society and not just within the pro-Palestine crowd. We're seeing Bushnell's final words about the US empire's complicity with genocide shared on mainstream networks like CNN and ABC, while Israel apologists run around falling all over themselves trying to tell people nobody cares about what Bushnell did like a guy sending a woman dozens of texts saying he's totally unbothered that she rejected his advances. A member of the US military lighting himself on fire while screaming "Free Palestine" is absolutely devastating to the information interests of Israel and the United States, because it shakes people awake like nothing else ever could.

All around our fake plastic dystopia people are now opening their eyes, saying "Wait, huh? That man did what? Why? I thought nothing matters but my comfort and my feelings and my small circle of people I care about? My country is complicit in a what now? Is it possible I've been missing something important?"

With his profound act of sincerity, Aaron Bushnell extended the world an invitation to a very different way of looking at life. An invitation to pierce through the veil of superficiality and narcissism to a radical authenticity and a deep compassion for our fellow human beings. To a profound sincerity of our own, with which we can shake the world awake in our own unique ways.

At 1 PM on February 25th, Aaron Bushnell lit more than one kind of fire. A fire that drives us to act. A fire that lights the way. A fire that inspires us. A fire that shows us another way of being. A fire which shows us a better world is possible.

We won't forget his message. We couldn't if we tried.

•

Israel Accused Of Torturing UN Workers To Obtain False Testimony About UNRWA

A recent UNRWA document says its staff report having been tortured while detained by Israeli forces, who pressed them to provide false statements about ties between the agency and Hamas.

"The document said several UNRWA Palestinian staffers had been detained by the Israeli army, and added that the ill-treatment and abuse they said they had experienced included severe physical beatings, waterboarding, and threats of harm to family members," Reuters reports, saying UNRWA workers "reported having been pressured by Israeli authorities into falsely stating that the agency has Hamas links and that staff took part in the Oct. 7 attacks."

This is another one of those stories about Israeli offenses that are so stunning that at first you can mistakenly believe you must not be reading it correctly—especially since the western political-media class haven't been treating it like the jarring news that it is. If we had anything remotely like an objective news media in the western world, reports that Israel tortured United Nations staff to get them to make false statements against a UN aid agency would be the top story everywhere for days.

Many, including myself, speculated that torture was involved in obtaining the Israeli "intelligence" behind initial claims of UNRWA staff involvement in the October 7 attack when this narrative first surfaced back in January. A senior Israeli official told Axios at the time that Israeli intelligence agencies came upon the information about the UNRWA staffers largely through "interrogations of militants who were arrested during the Oct. 7 attack." Israel has an extensive history of using torture in its interrogations, and there's no reason to believe such methods haven't been used on captured Hamas fighters in recent months—but reports that it was actual UN staff being tortured are something new.

We may be certain that if it was Hamas being accused of torturing workers for international aid agencies in order to extract false confessions, we'd never hear the end of it. To this day unsubstantiated rumors of mass systemic sexual violence on October 7 continue to dominate the headlines resulting in scandalous instances of

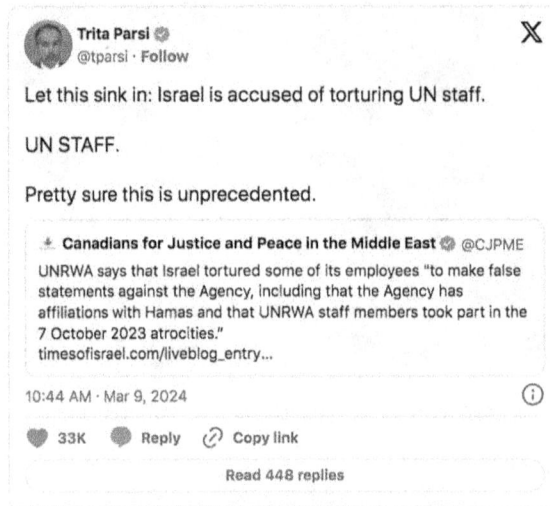

Trita Parsi ✅
@tparsi · Follow

Let this sink in: Israel is accused of torturing UN staff.

UN STAFF.

Pretty sure this is unprecedented.

> ⚜ **Canadians for Justice and Peace in the Middle East** ✅ @CJPME
> UNRWA says that Israel tortured some of its employees "to make false statements against the Agency, including that the Agency has affiliations with Hamas and that UNRWA staff members took part in the 7 October 2023 atrocities."
> timesofisrael.com/liveblog_entry...

10:44 AM · Mar 9, 2024

♡ 33K   Reply   Copy link

Read 448 replies

journalistic malpractice, despite the Israeli spinmeisters behind those reports having a much worse track record than UNRWA in the truth-telling department and UNRWA standing much less to gain than Israel by lying.

But that's what the information ecosystem looks like in the shadow of the empire. The flimsiest allegations against enemies of the US-centralized power alliance are spun as gospel truth and kept in the headlines for months, while even the most damning evidence against the empire never gets anything better than a cursory nod from the mass media and is then promptly memory-holed as the daily news churn moves on.

•

Crocodile Tears For Gaza While Backing Its Destruction

It says so much about US politics that Biden's most vulnerable political weak point is the fact that he's sponsoring a genocide, but Republicans can't attack him on that point because they support the genocide too.

•

It's amazing how fast the bill to ban TikTok is being shoved through by US lawmakers. This would easily be the single most significant act of direct government censorship in US history.

•

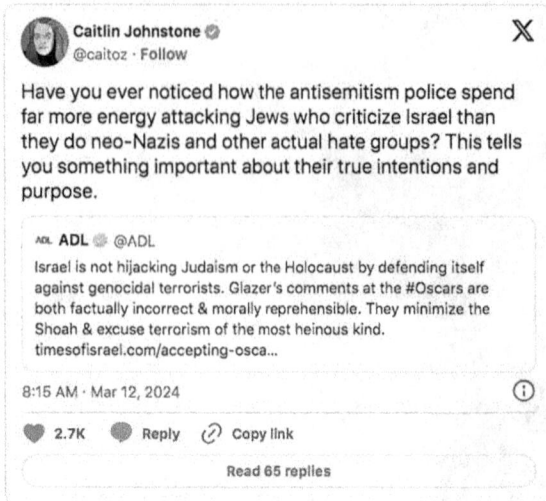

Caitlin Johnstone ✓
@caitoz · Follow

Have you ever noticed how the antisemitism police spend far more energy attacking Jews who criticize Israel than they do neo-Nazis and other actual hate groups? This tells you something important about their true intentions and purpose.

> ADL ✓ @ADL
>
> Israel is not hijacking Judaism or the Holocaust by defending itself against genocidal terrorists. Glazer's comments at the #Oscars are both factually incorrect & morally reprehensible. They minimize the Shoah & excuse terrorism of the most heinous kind.
> timesofisrael.com/accepting-osca...

8:15 AM · Mar 12, 2024

♡ 2.7K   💬 Reply   🔗 Copy link

Read 65 replies

Nothing's more enraging than seeing the western officials who are making this genocide possible weep crocodile tears about how "heartbreaking" it is. You're fucking doing it to them you shitstains! It's like beating someone to death while sobbing about how tragic their untimely death will be.

•

Israel's atrocities in Gaza are quantifiably much, much, much worse than October 7. We're begging the western press to give as much weight to the suffering inflicted upon Palestinians by the Gaza genocide as the suffering inflicted on Israelis by October 7, when in reality it deserves much, much more weight.

•

We're about two weeks out from seeing mass media reports like "Biden administration to begin airdropping child-sized coffins into Gaza to aid Palestinians in their unfortunate time of need."

•

Democrats: We stand for justice and equality and we oppose racism and oppression!

Palestinian: Oh so you oppose the genocide in Gaza then?

Democrats: Oh god no. No we meant, like, we want more Latinx landlords.

•

Saying it's racist and evil to criticize Zionists is like saying it's racist and evil to criticize conservatives. It's a fucking political ideology.

•

The thing is we don't know how to do this. We don't know how to keep eight billion homo sapiens alive without destroying the ecosystem. We don't know how eight billion humans can share the earth without wiping each other out via the armageddon weapons they invented. Without hurting, exploiting, oppressing and enslaving each other.

We've got some ideas about how this could be done, but we've never actually done it. In the extremely short amount of time this planet has had billions of humans on it, we've never come anywhere remotely close to figuring out how to avoid cataclysmic disaster and nightmarish dystopia. We're still very much on that trajectory, and because of the competition-based systems we have in place, nothing is happening to steer us away.

So we are all—every single one of us—right now doing something that we don't know how to do. We are living on this planet, but we don't actually know how to. We are one of eight billion humans who don't know how to sustain a world of eight billion humans. We're in the water, but we don't know how to swim.

And we could all probably use a little bit of humility about this. Everywhere we look we see pundits, politicians and thought leaders talking about what changes need to be made to our society and our world in confident-sounding voices, but none of them actually know. The very best of them have some educated guesses as to how we might start making the necessary changes to avoid various disasters, but since we haven't even started making any real changes, they don't actually know. We're a bunch of lost little kids who can't find their parents.

Obviously we need to learn how to swim, because these are the waters we were birthed into. I mean only to say here that our collective efforts to learn how to swim would probably be aided by a lot more curiosity about how swimming might actually occur and what it would actually look like, and a lot less confident-sounding bloviation from people who've never swam an inch in their lives.

A humble curiosity about this entirely unprecedented situation we've found ourselves in would probably serve our species well.

Featured image via Rawpixel.

Saying "Hamas Just Needs To Surrender" Is Saying "We'll Kill Kids Until We Get What We Want"

Of the many awful warmonger comments President Biden made in his State of the Union address Thursday night, arguably the worst was when he reiterated the US empire's position that it is fine and good for the IDF to keep murdering Gazan civilians until Hamas bows to all of Israel's demands.

Biden did this by lamenting the "heartbreaking" death and starvation of civilians in Gaza while in the same breath stating that Hamas could end all of this violence by laying down arms and surrendering those responsible for the October 7 attack.

"Israel has a right to go after Hamas," Biden said. "Hamas ended this conflict by releasing the hostages, laying down arms—could end it by—by releasing the hostages, laying down arms, and surrendering those responsible for October 7th."

"This war has taken a greater toll on innocent civilians than all previous wars in Gaza combined," Biden went on to say. "More than 30,000 Palestinians have been killed, most of whom are not Hamas. Thousands and thousands of innocents—women and children. Girls and boys also orphaned. Nearly 2 million more Palestinians under bombardment or displacement. Homes destroyed, neighborhoods in rubble, cities in ruin. Families without food, water, medicine."

"It's heartbreaking," added Biden, referring to the genocide that he himself is actively backing and could choose to end at any time.

(Democrats love babbling about how "heartbreaking" Gaza is. It's their favorite thing to do. They love nothing more than to weep publicly over the death and starvation and unfathomable human suffering they themselves are directly responsible for, as though it's some kind of natural disaster and not a US-backed genocide that is only happening because this Democrat-run administration actively facilitates it.)

We don't talk enough about how horrifyingly evil it is that the actual, stated position of Israel and its immensely powerful allies is that all of the killing and starvation of Palestinian civilians in Gaza is entirely the fault of Hamas, because Hamas has not acquiesced to the military demands made by Israel. In effect, it is saying "We will kill thousands and thousands of children until you give us everything we want."

I mean, imagine if Russia did that. Imagine if Putin started raining military explosives on parts of Ukraine known to be densely packed with children, and then saying the mass-scale child-killing will continue until Ukraine surrenders and that all of the child deaths are actually the fault of the Ukrainians because they still haven't given Putin everything he wants.

I think we all know that if such a thing were to happen it would be the subject of worldwide condemnation, and justifiably so. Such a tactic is not meaningfully different from lining up children on their knees on the battlefield and shooting them one by one in the back of the head until the enemy unconditionally surrenders.

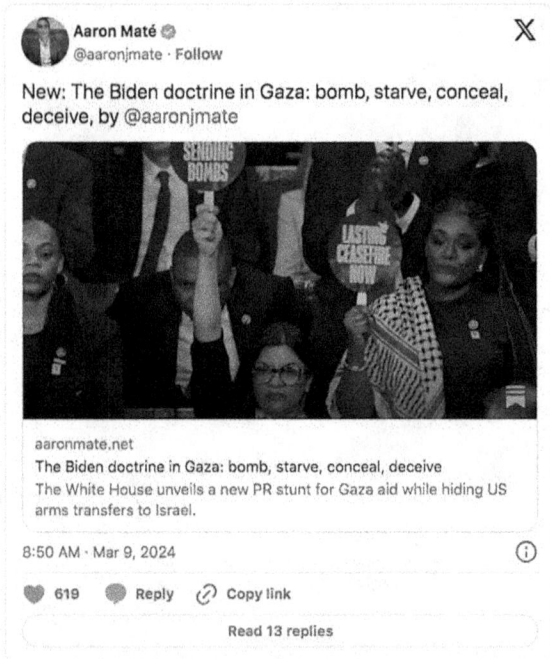

Aaron Maté ✓
@aaronjmate · Follow

New: The Biden doctrine in Gaza: bomb, starve, conceal, deceive, by @aaronjmate

aaronmate.net
The Biden doctrine in Gaza: bomb, starve, conceal, deceive
The White House unveils a new PR stunt for Gaza aid while hiding US arms transfers to Israel.

8:50 AM · Mar 9, 2024

619   Reply   Copy link
Read 13 replies

They're not just doing this with airstrikes and bullets—they're doing it with food as well. Aaron Maté has a new article out titled "The Biden doctrine in Gaza: bomb, starve, deceive" which picks apart statements from White House officials about the temporary pier this administration is planning to build on Gaza's coast over the next several weeks, ostensibly to allow for the arrival of more aid into the enclave.

Maté writes the following:

"The US military pier, Biden claimed, 'will enable a massive increase in the amount of humanitarian assistance getting into Gaza every day.' His own aides acknowledge that this is a ruse. According to the Washington Post, administration officials quietly concede that 'only by securing the opening of additional land crossings would there be enough aid to prevent famine.' And given that the pier will take at minimum 30 days to complete, that '[raises] questions about how famine in Gaza will be staved off in the critical days ahead,' the New York Times notes.

"The White House has given the answer: rather than compel Israel to open those land crossings and prevent famine, it is instead adopting the Israeli position that the land crossings can be used as a tool of leverage against Hamas—and that Israel can control everything that gets in. In ceasefire talks, Israel has demanded that Hamas release hostages in exchange for, at best, a six-week pause to the massacre."

Maté explains that Vice President Kamala Harris recently gave a speech in which she said Hamas needs to agree to a hostage deal in order to "get a significant amount of aid in," which is the same as saying Israel and its allies will help starve Gazan civilians until Hamas capitulates to their demands.

"The very fact that the delivery of 'a significant amount' of aid is conditional on Hamas accepting Israeli demands underscores that Israel, with US backing, is using that aid as a tool of coercion," Maté writes, noting that this directly contradicts Biden's admonishment to Israeli leaders in his State of the Union address that "Humanitarian assistance cannot be a secondary consideration or a bargaining chip."

Washington's role in the mass murder of Palestinians in Gaza makes a lot more sense when you stop looking at it as a reluctant passive witness to Israel's crimes and begin viewing it as an active participant. US officials will occasionally wag their fingers at the Netanyahu government and act like Israel's worst atrocities are being carried out against the beneficent humanitarian wishes of the United States, but if you mentally mute all the narrative spin that's being placed on this thing you just see a giant concentration camp packed full of children being murdered at mass scale by the most powerful empire that has ever existed.

Featured image via Picryl.

Genocidal Psychopaths Celebrate International Day To Combat Islamophobia

Well it's International Day to Combat Islamophobia, which of course means Democrats are busy making the most hypocritical and morally dissonant public statements you can possibly imagine.

"We recognize the violence and hate that Muslims worldwide too often face because of their religious beliefs—and the ugly resurgence of Islamophobia in the wake of the devastating war in Gaza," reads a statement from President Biden, referring to a US-backed genocide against a Muslim population that he is personally responsible for.

"Today, as millions continue to observe the holy month of Ramadan, Jill and I extend our best wishes to Muslims everywhere and continue to keep them in our prayers. And, we reaffirm our commitment to do all we can to put an end to the vicious hate of Islamophobia—here at home and around the world," concludes the statement from the president now known internationally as Genocide Joe.

"On this International Day to Combat Islamophobia, we reaffirm our commitment to upholding the freedom of religion or belief of all and to speak out against acts of anti-Muslim hatred whenever and wherever they occur," adds Secretary of State Antony Blinken.

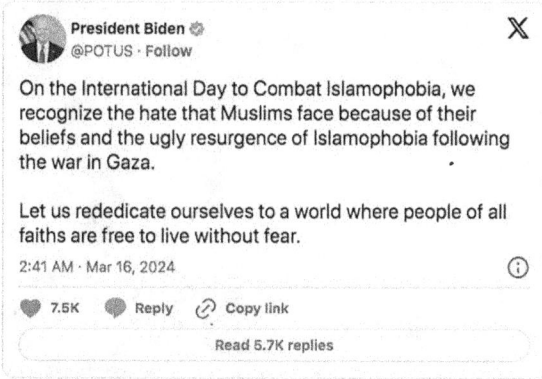

"Islamophobia has no place in our nation and around the world. POTUS and I join the world in condemning Islamophobia and affirming the equal rights and dignity of all people," tweets Vice President Kamala Harris.

This is so creepy. It's one of those things where the more you look at it, the creepier it becomes. They're condemning Islamophobia and denouncing hate crimes against Muslims at the exact same time as they are helping Israel create a mountain of Palestinian corpses in a genocidal onslaught whose entire premise is that Palestinians are the wrong race and the wrong religion. They are proclaiming their love for the Muslim while plunging a knife into his throat.

But that's exactly who Democrats are. Their actions don't matter, only their feelings matter. It didn't matter that Obama expanded all of Bush's most depraved wars and butchered Muslim populations using bombs and proxy militias throughout his entire administration, all that mattered was that he spoke eloquently and expressed compassion when the cameras were on. It doesn't matter that Biden is directly backing a genocidal campaign which has probably killed far more people than the official death counts acknowledge, it matters that he condemns Islamophobia and that White House sources keep feeding the press stories about how privately "frustrated" he is with Benjamin Netanyahu. The whole thing's just a vehicle through which the more progressively-minded half of the American public can support the murderous agendas of the US empire while still feeling nice about themselves.

Republicans are the openly fascistic thugs of the US empire, while Democrats are the the psychopathic PR managers running around photoshopping smiley faces on the fascism. Republicans are the dopey goon squad, while Democrats are the criminal mastermind. Republicans are the blunt instrument, while Democrats are the poison syringe. Republicans kill Muslims while saying they hate Muslims, while Democrats kill Muslims while saying they love them.

Democrats are the grinning plastic mask that sits on top of the snarling, blood-spattered face of the US empire. They purport to stand in solidarity with workers, with marginalized groups, with women and with the poor, and they claim to oppose racism, injustice and tyranny, but when it comes right down to it their real purpose is to put a nice face on the most murderous and tyrannical regime on this planet.

•

• Notes From The Edge Of The Narrative Matrix •

• Notes From The Edge Of The Narrative Matrix •
They're Really Going To Try To Lay All The Blame For Gaza On Netanyahu

They're really going to try to pin all the blame for the incineration of Gaza on Benjamin Netanyahu so that nothing has to change when this is over. The western empire has chosen a single scapegoat to carry away its sins so the status quo can march on unhindered by guilt or consequence.

They want everyone to pin all the blame for the Gaza genocide on Netanyahu, but this is not all the fault of Netanyahu. It's the fault of the entire Israeli state. It's the fault of Joe Biden. It's the fault of the Democrats. It's the fault of all the Israel supporters on Capitol Hill. It's the fault of the western press. It's the fault of the Israel lobby. It's the fault of the unelected empire managers in US government agencies. It's the fault of the entire US empire and all its imperial member states like Australia, the UK, the EU, and Canada.

By trying to make this mass atrocity solely the fault of Netanyahu and not the giant, sprawling network of immensely powerful institutions which made it possible, they're working to ensure that no changes will need to be made to any of those institutions. It's just like how they made a scapegoat of Judith

Miller for the entire mass media's war propaganda in the lead-up to the Iraq invasion and let all the blame for the war hang on Bush (before completely rehabilitating Bush's image during the Trump administration and deciding he's a pretty great guy after all). No meaningful changes were ever made to ensure that the US power alliance never repeats its horrible crimes after Iraq, which is why it keeps repeating horrible crimes.

•

The trouble with Israel apologia on Gaza is that at first glance its talking points sound legit if you don't know much about Israel-Palestine. "Israel has a right to defend itself", "They need to get rid Hamas because of October 7" etc would sound entirely reasonable if you didn't know that Israel is a settler-colonialist apartheid state who has been murdering, abusing and stealing from the indigenous population of the land for generations.

The amount of energy needed to see through the talking points is far greater than the amount of energy needed to speak them—it's one of those "A lie gets halfway around the world before the truth even gets its pants on" kind of deals. Which is why it's miraculous that so many people around the world are getting educated enough to see through the lies and support the Palestinians.

How are they getting educated enough? Mostly through online content which sums up the situation quickly and concisely enough for them to understand easily. That's the only way the truth can move quickly enough to catch up with the lies. And that's the role TikTok has played here, which is why we've seen Israel lobbyists and the ADL shrieking their lungs out about it for months.

•

It would never have occurred to any American to think TikTok is a five-alarm foreign enemy threat until their government told them to think that, and then when they did the biggest bootlickers in the world started acting like it's just a common sense fact they've always believed.

Americans who'd trust their own government to oversee their communications more than they'd trust China have missed all the most important lessons about the US government that have come out in their lives. Even if China really is getting data from TikTok (and there's currently no evidence that it is), only a groveling empire simp would object to it.

•

Saying TikTok must be suppressing pro-Israel content because pro-Palestine content is more popular is like saying they're suppressing flat earth content because round earth content is more popular. Pro-Israel content is just less popular in general, which is why the gap is the same on Facebook and Instagram.

•

The US government is like "No no it's not censorship, we're just using state power to ensure that popular speech platforms are only allowed to exist if they can be controlled by US government agencies."

•

Israel has done so much fucked up shit in the last few days we've already forgotten the news that they literally tortured UN staff to extract false statements about UNRWA having Hamas connections.

They. Tortured. UN. Staff. If we had anything remotely like objective news reporting in the western press, this would have been the top story everywhere for days.

•

Once you see how evil Israel's actions are you start to understand why its defenders need to resort to just calling anyone who criticizes Israel a Jew-hater.

•

When Israel apologists say "antisemite" it's just a meaningless noise made to hurt the feelings of the person it's said to. Once you realize this it starts to land in exactly the same way as any other infantile name-calling from anyone else who's lost the argument.

Featured image via Wikimedia Commons/President.gov.ua (CC BY 4.0 DEED)

You Can't Trust Any Part Of This Dystopia If You Want Health And Sanity

In a society where products are made to generate profit instead of wellbeing, you've got to be conscious and selective about what goes into you.

In a society where news media and punditry are produced based on the kind of ratings they will draw and how well they defend the powerful, you've got to be conscious and selective about what kinds of news media and punditry you let into your mind.

In a society where movies and shows are produced based on how much money they can make rather than how edifying and enriching they are, you've got to be conscious and selective about what movies and shows you let into your senses.

In a society where food is produced to make money rather than to promote wellbeing, you've got to be conscious and selective about what kinds of food you let into your body.

In a society where pharmaceuticals are produced to ensure continued profits rather than health, you've got to be conscious and selective about what pharmaceuticals you allow into your system.

In a society where products are manufactured to generate profits rather than to meet material needs, you've got to be conscious and selective about what products you let into your home.

In a society where even religion and spirituality are lucratively commodified, you've got to be conscious and selective about what spiritual belief systems you allow into your worldview.

We live in a very sick and crazy society, and if you're not conscious and selective about how you interact with every facet of it you'll inevitably get swept up in the sickness and craziness yourself. Health and wellbeing are still possible within the framework of our present dystopia, but you need to hold every part of it at arm's length and examine it with a critical eye before taking it in.

This civilization is not your friend. Hopefully someday we'll live in a civilization whose component parts we can trust, but this civilization is rife with poison for our bodies, our minds, and our hearts. And we need to conduct ourselves in accordance with this reality if we want to be healthy.

Featured image via Terabass (CC BY-SA 3.0)

Don't Equate The Violence Of The Oppressor With The Violence Of The Oppressed

Israel has once again stormed Gaza's al-Shifa Hospital. Israel spent the first few weeks of the Gaza assault churning out fake audio clips of Hamas fighters exonerating the IDF from attacking hospitals and healthcare workers, and has spent all the months since just unapologetically attacking hospitals and healthcare workers.

•

CNN's Dana Bash just gave an adoring rimjob of an interview to Benjamin Netanyahu, telling him "You're not Hamas. Israel is a democracy, and as a Jewish state supports and believes in every life mattering."

If Netanyahu was interviewed by an actual journalist he'd be forcefully interrogated with extremely uncomfortable questions about his genocidal atrocities in Gaza. When Netanyahu goes on CNN the anchor recites all of his pro-genocide talking points for him so he that doesn't have to.

•

The underlying assumption behind the claim that Hamas needs to be eliminated is that Israel should be able to inflict nonstop violence on Palestinians day after day, year after year, generation after generation, without ever receiving any violence in return.

•

You can't equate the violence of the oppressor with the violence of the oppressed. They're not the same, and the oppressor is the ultimate source of the violence from both sides.

Say you've got a group of blue guys and a group of green guys. If the blue guys have power over the green guys and are constantly oppressing them, stealing from them, using violence on them and generally making life intolerable for the people they have power over, then the blue guys have no moral standing to get indignant and outraged when the green guys start responding to this with their own violence. That would be a ridiculous and illogical position for anyone to take.

In fact, if you look at what happened in our hypotetical scenario here, the blue guys are morally responsible for both their own violence AND the violence of the green guys, because they created the dynamics in which both happened. Had the blue guys not been oppressing and abusing the green guys, the green guys would not have responded with violence.

And you can argue "But the green guys aren't making things any better with their violence! It's just making the blue guys madder and more violent!" But that's completely irrelevant to the question of responsibility, and to the fact that if the blue guys stop their violence and abuse there will be a cessation of violence from both sides.

The solution therefore is not to spend any energy whatsoever yelling at the green guys to stop being violent, the solution is to demand the blue guys stop being violent, abusive and oppressive toward the green guys—because that is the source of violence between the two groups. The violence of the blue guys is a cause, while the violence of the green guys is only an effect. You cannot therefore regard them in the same way, either morally or practically.

•

Niger kicking the French military out of the country was interesting and potentially significant. Niger kicking out both France and the US is a major development. To borrow a line from Django Unchained, gentlemen you had my curiosity, but now you have my attention.

•

The US is backing a genocide and waging a proxy war against a nuclear superpower while the American people struggle with stagnant wages, a broken healthcare system and soaring costs of living, so naturally Americans are being told they need to be very, very worried about China.

•

Right wingers who regard themselves as bold anti-establishment freethinkers are currently defending the world's most powerful government supplying bombs to drop on a giant concentration camp with arguments that ultimately boil down to "But the TV would never lie to me!"

•

If opposition to an active genocide shocks and offends you, that's a character flaw, and you should change that about yourself. If it shocks and offends you because of your religious identity, that too is a character flaw. Supporting mass murder because of your religion is not a legitimate position to have.

Featured image via Adobe Stock.

It's Journalistic Malpractice To Say Gazans Are Starving Without Saying Israel Is Starving Them

The mass media are printing some amazingly depraved headlines about a new UN-backed report on starvation in Gaza from the Integrated Food Security Phase Classification, who says half the enclave's population is now at the highest-possible threat level for starvation.

The New York Times has a real corker out titled "Famine Is Projected for Northern Gaza, Experts Say", subtitled "A global authority on food security said that in the coming months, as many as 1.1 million people in Gaza could face the severest levels of hunger."

A casual news consumer could get multiple paragraphs into this article assuming that people in a place called Gaza are suffering from some kind of famine caused by natural events, like a drought or something. Not until paragraph four would they encounter the word "Israeli", and not until paragraph five would they encounter the line "Israeli's bombardment and a near-total blockade."

At a time when only 20 percent of news readers ever make it past the headline of a given story, this is an extremely destructive and propagandistic act of journalistic malpractice. The editors of The New York Times know exactly what they're doing packaging a story about Israel's deliberate starvation of Palestinian civilians like it's a troubling prediction about the weather.

Contrast the New York Times' headline with that of Al Jazeera's report on the same story: "Gaza headed towards famine amid Israeli aid curbs: What to know". That's the normal way to present a story about a deliberately inflicted famine upon an imperiled population. If a population was being deliberately starved by siege warfare from a nation like Russia, China or Iran, we may be absolutely certain that the name of that nation would appear in the headline.

But because the western media exist to generate propaganda and not to report the news, we get headlines like "Gaza faces famine during Ramadan, the holy month of fasting" from the BBC, and "Famine in northern Gaza is imminent as more than 1 million people face 'catastrophic' levels of hunger, new report warns" from CNN, and "Famine imminent in northern Gaza, says UN-backed report" from Reuters, and "'Catastrophic levels of hunger' in Gaza mean famine is imminent, says aid coalition" from The Guardian.

We saw this with Saudi Arabia's US-backed starvation of Yemen as well. When the mass media talked about Yemen at all (usually they just ignored it), editors consistently obfuscated the fact that this was a population being deliberately starved by a cruel blockade and the deliberate targeting of food infrastructure. The fact that it was being made possible by the United States was almost never mentioned.

This is a very good example of how western propaganda works, by the way. The mainstream western press don't generally make up whole-cloth lies (though they will uncritically print claims made by western government agencies who have an extensive history of lying); what they do is rely on half-truths, distortions and lies by omission to give their audiences a wildly slanted picture of what's going on in the world. By always going out of their way to tell you an enemy of the US-centralized empire is committing an atrocity the millisecond it looks like they might be, while being furtive and obfuscatory about the crimes of the US and its allies, they give their audience a skewed understanding of who is and is not committing the real evils in our world.

This doesn't typically happen as a result of any grand monolithic conspiracy; it's mostly just the natural consequence of having all the major news platforms controlled by wealthy and powerful people who each have a vested interest in manufacturing consent for the status quo upon which their wealth and power are premised. The oligarchs control the media, and they hire the executives who run the media, and the executives hire the editors who write the headlines and guide the reporters to report a certain way, and this gives rise to a system where everyone working for the outlet conducts themselves in a way that just so happens to suit the powerful people on top.

Then before you know it you've got editors at The New York Times—a paper that's been published by the same family for over a century—packaging a story about starvation caused by an Israeli siege to look like it's a story about an innocent crop failure. Odds are nobody told them to do that; they just learned over the years that that's how you rise to the top in an outlet like The New York Times.

Featured image via Adobe Stock.

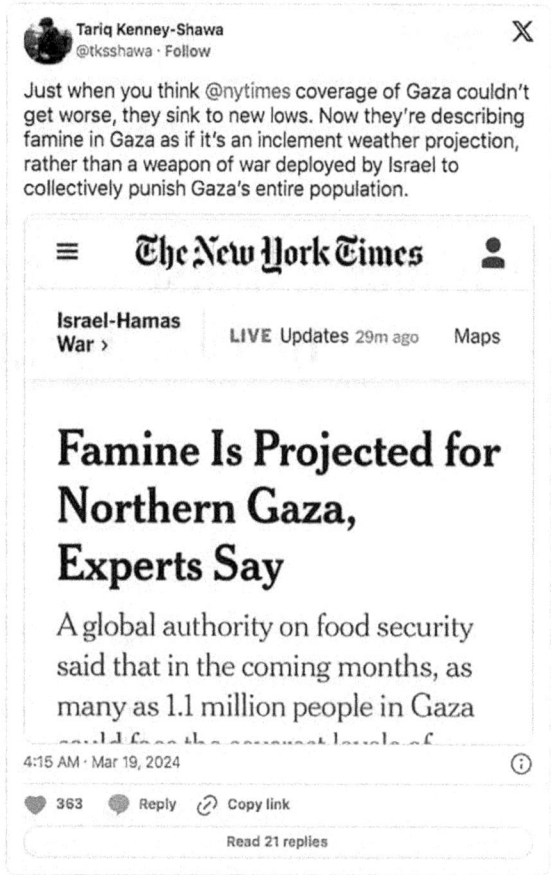

Tariq Kenney-Shawa
@tksshawa · Follow

Just when you think @nytimes coverage of Gaza couldn't get worse, they sink to new lows. Now they're describing famine in Gaza as if it's an inclement weather projection, rather than a weapon of war deployed by Israel to collectively punish Gaza's entire population.

The New York Times

Israel-Hamas War ›   LIVE Updates 29m ago   Maps

Famine Is Projected for Northern Gaza, Experts Say

A global authority on food security said that in the coming months, as many as 1.1 million people in Gaza

4:15 AM · Mar 19, 2024

363   Reply   Copy link

Read 21 replies

Without Extensive Narrative Manipulation, None Of This Would Be Consented To

Without extensive narrative manipulation, it would never occur to anyone that bombing Gaza into rubble is a reasonable response to a single Hamas attack.

Without extensive narrative manipulation, it would never occur to anyone that killing tens of thousands of Palestinians and starving hundreds of thousands more is a reasonable response to a thousand Israelis being killed.

Without extensive narrative manipulation, it would never occur to anyone that criticizing the actions of the state of Israel is antisemitic.

Without extensive narrative manipulation, it would never occur to anyone that saying "from the river to the sea" is a call for genocide.

Without extensive narrative manipulation, it would never occur to anyone to think about this onslaught and the discourse around it in terms of "Jews vs Jew haters".

Without extensive narrative manipulation, it would never occur to anyone that it was fine and normal to keep an unwanted ethnic group in a walled-in area whose resources are tightly controlled by those in power.

Without extensive narrative manipulation, it would never occur to anyone that TikTok is a massive problem that needs to be eliminated.

Without extensive narrative manipulation, it would never occur to anyone that Israel should be able to inflict violence and abuse upon the Palestinian population for generations without ever receiving any violence in return.

Without extensive narrative manipulation, it would never occur to anyone that Israel using the Israeli army to murder civilians in an Israeli military campaign is something that can be blamed on Hamas.

Without extensive narrative manipulation, it would never occur to anyone that it is fine and acceptable for the IDF to be targeting healthcare workers, journalists and scholars and destroying hospitals, universities and mosques.

Without extensive narrative manipulation, it would never occur to anyone that dozens of Israeli hostages are more important than the hundreds of thousands of Palestinians who are being starved and murdered.

Without extensive narrative manipulation, it would never occur to anyone that the US war machine should be bombing people in Yemen, Iraq and Syria to stop their retaliations for the destruction of Gaza.

Without extensive narrative manipulation, it would never occur to anyone that the governments who are backing a genocide are not personally responsible for it.

Without extensive narrative manipulation, it would never occur to anyone that the unfathomable suffering that is taking place in Gaza right now should not be at the forefront of our attention.

Without extensive narrative manipulation, it would never occur to anyone that the genocide in Gaza should be allowed to continue instead of being brought to an immediate end.

And that's why we've been seeing such extensive narrative manipulation—from our news media, from our government officials, and from Israel apologists on social media.

It's because without extensive narrative manipulation, none of this would be consented to.

Featured image via Wikimedia Commons (CC BY-SA 3.0 DEED)

Find Someone Who Loves You Like Israel Loves Attacking Palestinian Hospitals

The World Health Organization has issued a statement saying that it has recorded 410 Israeli attacks on Gazan healthcare services since October 7, resulting in 685 fatalities, 902 injuries, and damage to 99 healthcare facilities.

As of this writing there is a still-ongoing IDF assault on Al-Shifa Hospital, which according to Israel has resulted in scores of Palestinian deaths and the capture of hundreds of prisoners. This is the fourth time Israel has attacked this particular hospital, which happens to be the largest hospital in Gaza.

Survivors of the assault have told Euro-Med Human Rights Monitor that they repeatedly witnessed groups of prisoners being walked into the hospital morgue by IDF troops, then heard the sound of gunfire, then saw the IDF troops returning without the prisoners. Which is probably exactly what it would look and sound like if the IDF was conducting mass summary executions at Al-Shifa Hospital.

In an article for The Washington Post titled "How Biden became embroiled in a Gaza conflict with no end in sight" (the western press have an extensive track record of constantly framing US military aggressions as passive entanglements that the global superpower keeps innocently stumbling and bumbling its way into by accident), Yasmeen Abutaleb and John Hudson report that according to their sources the Biden White House misrepresented the intelligence whose claims were used to justify the first Al-Shifa raid back in November.

Senator Chris Van Hollen, a Democrat, told The Washington Post that there was a marked discrepancy between what White House officials were saying publicly about Al-Shifa and what the intelligence they'd seen actually said:

"Van Hollen, who had received a classified briefing about the U.S. intelligence on al-Shifa, said there were 'important and subtle differences' between what Biden officials were saying publicly and what the intelligence actually showed. 'I did find there to be some disconnect between the administration's public statements and the classified findings,' the senator said."

In December, when it was all long over, The Washington Post published a report which found that "the evidence presented by the Israeli government falls short of showing that Hamas had been using the hospital as a command and control center." It was obvious that Israel was lying about Al-Shifa at the time back in November, with psyops like a nonexistent Hamas calendar being "discovered" in the hospital and a fake video purporting to show an Al-Shifa nurse saying the hospital was overrun with Hamas fighters being debunked as fast as they could be produced.

The evidence for the justification of this raid doesn't appear to be any more robust, with the IDF publishing highly dubious footage of what it claims are "Hamas terrorist funds found inside Shifa Hospital", complete with notes accompanying the money thanking Hamas by name for their "good work".

Sulaiman Ahmed ✓
@ShaykhSulaiman · Follow

BREAKING: ISRAEL TAKE MORE CIVILIANS HOSTAGE FROM AL-SHIFA

They took 160 palestinians hostage including;

☑ Intensive Unit Team
☑ Dr. Nihad Abed
☑ Dr. Mu'nis Muhaisen
☑ Senior Nurse Rohi Labban
☑ Nurse Kamal Kishko
☑ Orthopaedic Team
☑ Dr. Murad Al-Quqa
☑ Nurse Yosef Abo... Show more

2:17 AM · Mar 21, 2024

♥ 7.3K   Reply   Copy link

Read 246 replies

Yeah okay sure, people have been somehow sending "Dear Hamas" letters to the militant group with wads of cash enclosed, and Hamas has been keeping both the cash and the letters in Al-Shifa Hospital, where they were kind enough to leave it for the incoming IDF raid to discover. Sounds legit. Definitely not the sort of thing Israel has been caught lying about many times before.

Israel's constant fixation on attacking healthcare facilities makes no sense from a military strategic point of view, but it makes plenty of sense from a genocidal point of view. Hospitals are where people are brought to save their lives after they've been badly injured or have become acutely malnourished or sick, and they're where civilians would normally take shelter when nowhere else is safe.

All the way back in December we were already seeing reports that Gaza's healthcare system has been effectively destroyed by the nonstop attacks on healthcare facilities and the siege warfare cutting the enclave off from much-needed medical supplies. Now we are seeing Israel repeatedly re-attacking those same facilities, ensuring that they remain non-functioning despite all the most resilient efforts of the people of Gaza to stay alive.

This is exactly what it looks like. The narrative managers of Israel and the west will try to spin and distort the information you're seeing right in front of your face to try and make you believe you're seeing something other than what you're seeing, but the truth really couldn't be more self-evident. This is a genocide. If it wasn't, Israel wouldn't be methodically destroying hospitals while bombing and starving the population they've been oppressing for generations.

Featured image via Adobe Stock.

Caitlin Johnstone ✅
@caitoz · Follow

Are people not tired of having their intelligence insulted?

Israel Defense Forces ✅ @IDF

Operational Update: Hamas terrorist funds found inside Shifa Hospital.

Along with the funds themselves were notes thanking the Hamas and Islamic Jihad terrorists for their "good work".

Watch and see for yourselves:

11:14 AM · Mar 19, 2024

11.6K   Reply   Copy link

Read 199 replies

When The Imperial Media Report On An Israeli Massacre

In what many are now calling the Flour Massacre, at least 112 Gazans were killed and hundreds more injured after Israeli forces opened fire on civilians who were waiting for food from much-needed aid trucks near Gaza City on Thursday.

Initial investigations by Euro-Med Human Rights Monitor found that the crowd was fired upon by both IDF automatic rifles and by Israeli tanks, and that dozens of gunshot victims were hospitalized after the incident.

Israel's version of events has of course changed over the course of the day as narrative managers figure out how best to frame publicly available information in a way that doesn't harm Israel's PR interests. Currently we're at Israel admitting that IDF troops did indeed fire upon the crowd after previously denying this, but claiming that this isn't what caused most of the the casualties, saying it was actually the Palestinians trampling each other in a human "stampede" which caused them harm. Essentially the current argument is "Yes we shot them, but that's not why they died."

The IDF claims Israeli troops only began firing on the Palestinians because the soldiers "felt threatened" by them, which goes to show that there is no atrocity Israel could possibly commit where it wouldn't frame itself as the victim. Israel's Minister of National Security Itamar Ben-Gvir took the opportunity to praise the IDF for heroically fighting off the dangerous Palestinians and to argue that the incident proves it's too dangerous to keep allowing aid trucks into Gaza.

As terrible as the Israeli spin machine has been on this atrocity, the western imperial media have been even worse. The verbal gymnastics they've been performing in their headlines to avoid saying Israel massacred starving people who were waiting for food would be genuinely impressive if it wasn't so ghoulish.

"As Hungry Gazans Crowd a Convoy, a Crush of Bodies, Israeli Gunshots and a Deadly Toll" reads one New York Times header, like the summary of an episode of a Netflix murder mystery show.

"Chaotic aid delivery turns deadly as Israeli, Gazan officials trade blame," says an indecipherably cryptic headline from The Washington Post.

"Biden says Gaza food aid-related deaths complicate ceasefire talks," says The Guardian. "Food aid-related deaths"? Seriously?

"More than 100 killed as crowd waits for aid, Hamas-run health ministry says," reads a BBC headline. The UK's state broadcaster is here using a tried and true tactic for casting doubt on death counts by deliberately associating them with Hamas, despite the fact that the Gaza health ministry's death counts are considered so reliable that Israeli intelligence services use them in their own internal records.

"At least 100 killed and 700 injured in chaotic incident" says CNN, like it's describing a frat party that got out of control.

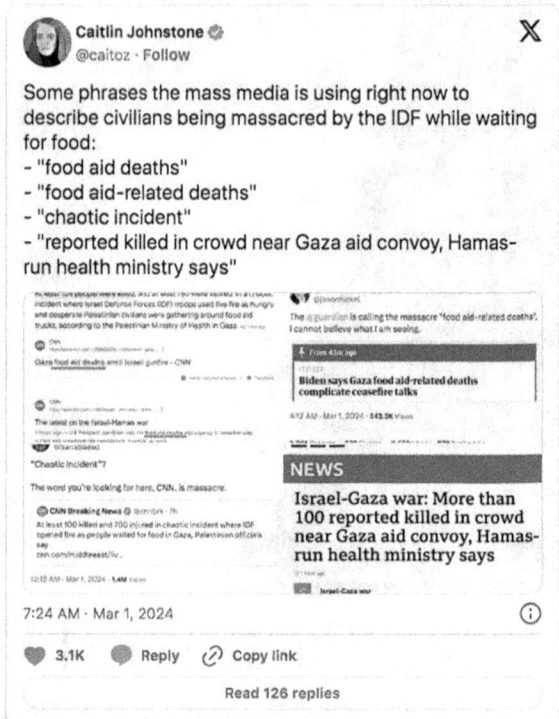

"Carnage at Gaza food aid site amid Israeli gunfire" reads another CNN headline, as though the carnage and the Israeli gunfire are two unrelated phenomena which just unluckily occurred at around the same time.

CNN also repeatedly refers to the killings as "food aid deaths", as though it's the food aid that killed them and not the military of a very specific and very nameable state power.

(It's probably worth noting at this point that CNN staff have been anonymously reporting through other outlets that there's been a uniquely aggressive top-down push within the network to slant reporting heavily in favor of Israeli information interests, driven largely by the new CEO Mark Thompson.)

So that's what happens when the imperial media report on an Israeli massacre, in case you were curious and haven't been paying attention since October 7 or the decades which preceded it. The propaganda services of the western press operate in a way that is typically indistinguishable from the spinmeistering of officials in western governments, framing the western empire and its allies in a positive light and their enemies in a negative one.

This happens because the western mass media do not exist to report the news and give you information about what's been going on in the world, but to manufacture consent for the political status quo and the globe-dominating power structure it supports. The only difference between our propaganda and the propaganda of a ruthless dictatorship is that the people who live under a dictatorship know they are being fed propaganda, whereas westerners are trained to believe they are ingesting impartial factual reporting.

The demolition of Gaza is alerting more and more westerners to the fact that this is happening, though, because the more blatant the atrocities the more ham-fisted the propaganda machine needs to be about running cover for them. It's even opening eyes within the propaganda machine itself, which is why we're seeing things like CNN staff blowing the whistle on their own CEO and New York Times staff telling The Intercept that their bosses committed extremely egregious journalistic malpractice in producing atrocity propaganda alleging mass rapes by Hamas on October 7.

The only good thing about what's happening in Gaza is that it's waking westerners up to the fact that everything they've been told about their society, their media and their world is a lie. Cracks are appearing in the illusion, and those of us who care about truth, peace and justice need to help draw attention to them. From there, real change becomes a genuine possibility.

Featured image via Adobe Stock.

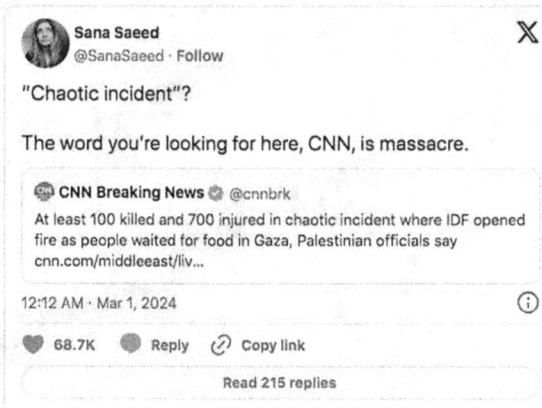

Sana Saeed
@SanaSaeed · Follow

"Chaotic incident"?

The word you're looking for here, CNN, is massacre.

> **CNN Breaking News** @cnnbrk
> At least 100 killed and 700 injured in chaotic incident where IDF opened fire as people waited for food in Gaza, Palestinian officials say
> cnn.com/middleeast/liv...

12:12 AM · Mar 1, 2024

The Empire's Weakness Is That It Still Needs Normal People To Turn Its Gears

Imperial propaganda outlet The New York Times is currently embroiled in a massive scandal over its reporting which alleges mass rapes on October 7 — and the scandal is being fueled in part by leaks from its own staff.

In case you haven't been following the story, back in December the Times published an article titled "'Screams Without Words': How Hamas Weaponized Sexual Violence on Oct. 7" which was riddled with glaring plot holes that were exposed by research from outlets like The Grayzone, Electronic Intifada, and Mondoweiss. Later it came out with the help of an anonymous Twitter account named zei_squirrel that one of the three authors of the New York Times piece—Anat Schwartz—is a genocide-supporting Israeli intelligence veteran who had never worked in journalism before, and that another author of the piece—a food writer named Adam Sella—is her partner's nephew.

In late January a report from The Intercept revealed that there was a major internal conflict at The New York Times about the strength of the reporting in "Screams Without Words", with a Times podcast dedicated to the article postponed and then abandoned when staff couldn't agree whether to stick to the original reporting and risk an embarrassing retraction, or present it in less certain light and tacitly advertise that they didn't have confidence in their report.

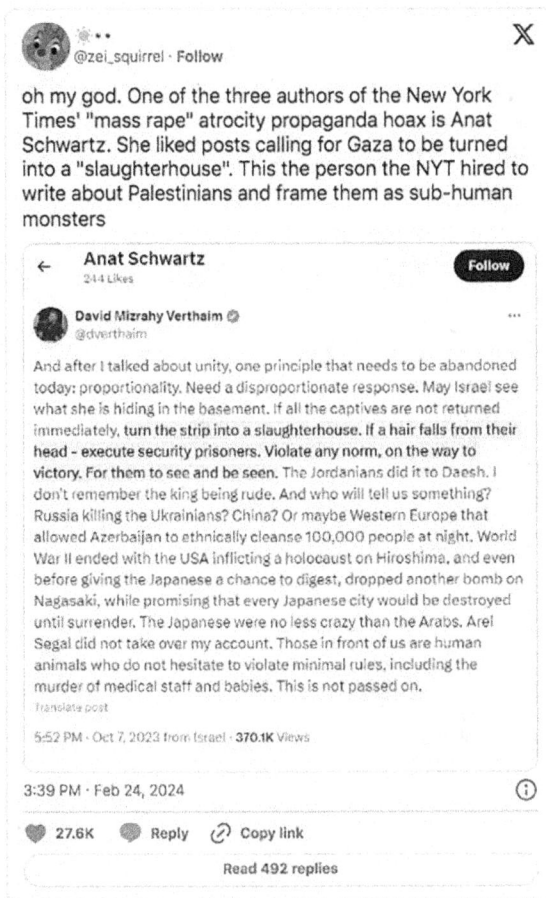

@zei_squirrel · Follow

oh my god. One of the three authors of the New York Times' "mass rape" atrocity propaganda hoax is Anat Schwartz. She liked posts calling for Gaza to be turned into a "slaughterhouse". This the person the NYT hired to write about Palestinians and frame them as sub-human monsters

Anat Schwartz
244 Likes

Follow

David Mizrahy Verthaim @
@dverthaim

And after I talked about unity, one principle that needs to be abandoned today: proportionality. Need a disproportionate response. May Israel see what she is hiding in the basement. If all the captives are not returned immediately, turn the strip into a slaughterhouse. If a hair falls from their head - execute security prisoners. Violate any norm, on the way to victory. For them to see and be seen. The Jordanians did it to Daesh. I don't remember the king being rude. And who will tell us something? Russia killing the Ukrainians? China? Or maybe Western Europe that allowed Azerbaijan to ethnically cleanse 100,000 people at night. World War II ended with the USA inflicting a holocaust on Hiroshima, and even before giving the Japanese a chance to digest, dropped another bomb on Nagasaki, while promising that every Japanese city would be destroyed until surrender. The Japanese were no less crazy than the Arabs. Arel Segal did not take over my account. Those in front of us are human animals who do not hesitate to violate minimal rules, including the murder of medical staff and babies. This is not passed on.

Translate post

5:52 PM · Oct 7, 2023 from Israel · 370.1K Views

3:39 PM · Feb 24, 2024

27.6K   Reply   Copy link

Read 492 replies

The other day The Intercept printed a follow-up piece which included more information from New York Times sources, as well as damning admissions Schwartz made in Hebrew on an Israeli podcast about the process of publishing "Screams Without Words". Schwartz's comments make it clear that everywhere she looked at the beginning of her investigation turned up zero evidence of sexual assault, only finding "evidence" when she moved on to thoroughly discredited sources like the ultra-orthodox group Zaka. It also makes it clear that it was The New York Times who approached Schwartz to help write "Screams Without Words" of their own initiative—so this scandal is all theirs.

In response to the leaks in the first Intercept article, The New York Times has launched a major leak investigation to determine who disclosed the information about internal strife at the paper to outside sources. Multiple anonymous New York Times staffers told Vanity Fair's Charlotte Klein that they couldn't remember any such inquisition having taken place before, and that they found it disconcerting.

"It's not something we do," a source told Klein. "That kind of witch hunt is really concerning."

So not only are New York Times staff leaking information about internal strife behind the scenes at the paper, they're also leaking information about the investigation into those leaks.

And now the Times Guild has sent a letter to New York Times publisher AG Sulzberger (whose family has published the paper for over a century), claiming NYT management have been singling out Arab and Muslim staff for interrogation on suspicion of leaking the information. Just imagine the outrage if a news outlet was explicitly singling out Jews on suspicion of betraying its interests over a story relating to Israel.

This is happening because the propaganda necessary to run cover for an active genocide diverges so wildly from what journalists have been trained to expect from a news outlet that even the fairly establishment-loyal staff of the mainstream press are becoming alarmed by it. The New York Times' coverage of Israel's destruction of Gaza has been so blatantly biased in favor of US and Israeli information interests that it's starting to shake people awake within the outlet itself—people whose unofficial job is to write propaganda for the US-centralized empire.

This is one of the weaknesses of the empire: that it depends on ordinary people to turn the gears of its institutions, and those ordinary people have been lied to about what those institutions are and what they do. We saw this illustrated recently in the self-immolation of Aaron Bushnell, who according to his friend Levi Pierpont initially joined the US Air Force to get out there and see the world but was quickly radicalized by what he saw on the inside of the US war machine. We've also seen this with the way CNN staff have been feeding information to other outlets about the network's policies of pro-Israel bias, and with the internal protests and resignations in the Biden administration over Gaza.

The western empire cannot operate without (A) ordinary people and

(B) nonstop lies and propaganda, and the more overt and ham-fisted (B) becomes the more it's necessarily going to conflict with its need for (A). The empire is going to struggle to get people dropping its bombs, moving its war machinery, churning out its propaganda and running its government agencies if it keeps acting in ways which dramatically conflict with what westerners have been taught to believe about their society, their media, their government, and their world.

This is why you'll sometimes see the empire step back from taking the most horrific actions it could take. It doesn't happen because the empire is moral or kind, it happens because it can't afford to wake too many people up to its depravity. That's the line the empire has been tightrope-walking these last five months, and the more attention we ordinary people can draw to the conflict between its actions and its narratives about itself, the more we shake that slender wire its feet struggle to balance upon.

Featured image via Adobe Stock.

You Have Already Taken A Side On Israel–Palestine (Whether You Admit It Or Not)

You have already taken a side on Israel-Palestine. Whether you know it or not. Whether you admit it or not.

You have either consciously chosen to side with the people who are being continually massacred by Israel, or you have consciously chosen to side with Israel, or you have sided with Israel by being "neutral", or you have sided with Israel by being indifferent.

As Desmond Tutu said, "If you are neutral in situations of injustice, you have chosen the side of the oppressor. If an elephant has its foot on the tail of a mouse, and you say that you are neutral, the mouse will not appreciate your neutrality."

The powerful oppressors are more than happy for you to be "neutral". The ones who are already in control want as little scrutiny as possible. From their position the fewer people who are looking them and evaluating whether their actions are right or wrong, the better. Your neutrality just means they get to keep doing what they want to do.

It's perfectly okay not to have an opinion about everything. It's fine not to take a position on every political issue that comes across your screen. Most people have way too many opinions, and most of them are about silly and unworthy things.

The onslaught that is happening in Gaza is not one such instance, though. Taking a stand against genocide is what having opinions on things is for. Opposing mass-scale human butchery and ethnic cleansing is the fundamental, bare-minimum position that all other political positions should follow from. If you can't take a stand against that, what are you even doing here? How have you been spending your brief time on this planet? How have you managed to make it to this point in life without maturing to the barest minimum standard possible?

You might think Israel-Palestine is too complicated for you to take a stand on. It isn't. It's very simple. Many of the small specific details are complex, but the overall reality they form is simple: an apartheid state has spent five months butchering and starving the population it has marginalized in a way that advances that state's longstanding political agendas of ethnically cleansing that population from the land.

You might think you're too cool or too evolved or too smart to take a side on Israel-Palestine. You are not. You have already taken a side, whether you admit it or not.

You might think Israel-Palestine has too many gray areas and uncertainties for you to legitimately take a side. It does not. The endless stream of footage of skeletal bodies and children ripped apart by military explosives over the last five months makes it very clear that this issue has a right side and a wrong side, and you are already standing on one of them.

By all means refuse to take sides on other issues; not taking a side is entirely legitimate when it comes to most issues people are wasting their breath bickering about. But not this one. When it comes to Gaza, reality demands a position from you.

That doesn't mean you have to side with the Palestinians if you don't want to. You are a sovereign human being; it's up to you. But don't kid yourself about being neutral. At least be real with yourself that by refusing to pick a position you are licking the boot of a nuclear-armed ethnostate that is backed by the most powerful empire the world has ever seen. If you can't be real about anything else, at least be real about that.

Featured image via Adobe Stock.

Aaron Bushnell's Death Can't Rightly Be Called An Act Of Suicide

There's a deeply moving interview on Democracy Now with a friend of Aaron Bushnell, the US airman who fatally self-immolated outside the Israeli embassy while screaming "Free Palestine" in protest of his government's facilitation of the genocide in Gaza.

Bushnell's friend, a conscientious objector named Levi Pierpont, met Bushnell in 2020 during basic training at an air force base in Texas. When you watch the interview you can immediately see why the two clicked; Pierpont has the same tender, gentle air to him that Bushnell displayed in his final video, very much unlike what you picture when you think of members of the world's most murderous and destructive military. Neither of them belonged there, and they each took their exit in their own way.

Toward the end of the interview, longtime Democracy Now host Amy Goodman asked Pierpont a question which drew an answer that's worth highlighting and reflecting upon.

"Would Aaron have described this as suicide?" Goodman asked Pierpont.

"No, absolutely not," Pierpont replied, adding, "He didn't have thoughts of suicide. He had thoughts of justice. That's what this was about. It wasn't about his life. It was about using his life to send a message."

This point is worthy of our consideration at this time because as soon as it became clear what Aaron Bushnell had done and the impact it was having on our collective consciousness, there was a mad rush to pathologize his act of protest and frame it as something other than what it was. The phrase "glorifying suicide" came up over and over again from Israel apologists desperate to mitigate the damage Bushnell's act had done to US and Israeli information interests, and we constantly saw Bushnell described as mentally ill and suicidal by spinmeisters acting in bad faith.

What Bushnell did isn't what people think of when they hear the word "suicide". It's not the sort of thing suicide prevention hotlines are set up to deter. It's not what mental health clinics are built to prevent. It's not what the designation "suicidal" is intended to point to.

When you say someone is suicidal, you are saying they don't want to be alive anymore and are in the process of making plans to bring about that result. They want to kill themselves because, in whatever way and for whatever reason, it hurts to live.

That isn't what happened with Aaron Bushnell. There is no indication that he was mentally unwell, or under any psychological stress beyond that which was inflicted upon him by the moral quandary of being a member of a war machine that is backing an active genocide. From what we can tell about his internal state given the information available to us, Bushnell would have been perfectly happy to go on living. He just prioritized peace and justice over his own life. He was no more suicidal than a rescue worker who died trying to save the lives of others.

In the case of suicide as we conventionally understand it, death is the goal. It is the both the means and the end, in and of itself. Bushnell's self-immolation was a means to a very different end: a free Palestine and the cessation of an ongoing genocide.

Such an act can't rightly be lumped in with those who kill themselves because they can't bear to go on living. It is different in every meaningful way. It is different in how it is experienced. It is different in how we should regard it as a society. It is different in its goals. It is different in its effects. The only thing it has in common with the conventional understanding of suicide is that it was brought about by one's own hand.

I don't enjoy quibbling about definitions or playing pedantic word games. Those who wish to frame what Aaron Bushnell did will object that it was a suicide per the technical dictionary definition, and they can feel as correct in doing so as they want to feel. My point here is that their continued use of that word in this context is done in bad faith, and in a way that is not conducive to truth and understanding. Far more conducive to truth and understanding would be to call what Bushnell did exactly what he himself called it: an extreme act of protest.

I will leave you with a quote that's been rattling around in my head these last few days by Ita Ford, an American Catholic nun who in 1980 was raped and murdered by a US-backed death squad in El Salvador:

"I hope that you come to find that which gives life a deep meaning for you. Something worth living for—maybe even worth dying for. Something that energizes you, enthuses you, enables you to keep moving ahead. I can't tell you what it might be—that's for you to find, to choose, to love. I can just encourage you to start looking and support you in the search."

Featured image via Elvert Barnes (CC BY-SA 2.0)

On Palestine And The Worthlessness Of The Western Liberal

There's an infuriatingly common type of liberal who purports to oppose Israel's actions in Gaza while also saying they support "Israel's right to exist", as though Israel's existence is somehow separable from its genocidal murderousness. This is a state that literally cannot exist without nonstop violence and tyranny, as demonstrated by its entire unbroken history since its inception. It was set up as a settler-colonialist outpost for western imperialism from the very beginning, and that's exactly what it's been ever since.

History has conclusively established that it is not possible to drop an artificial ethnostate on top of an already-existing population in which the pre-existing population is legally subordinate to the new one without tremendous amounts of warfare, police violence, mass displacement, apartheid, disenfranchisement and oppression. This is not actually debatable. It is a settled matter (no pun intended).

Is it possible to have a nation in which Jews are welcomed and kept safe? Of course. Many such nations exist outside of Israel, and the majority of the world's Jews live in them. What isn't possible is a Jewish ethnostate in historic Palestine in which the pre-existing population is treated as less than the Jewish population that does not necessarily entail nonstop violence, tyranny and abuse. This is self-evidently a direct contradiction in goals, but it's what the liberals we're discussing here pretend to believe is a reasonable possibility.

There absolutely could be a state in that region wherein Palestinians and Jews coexist peacefully, but it would be so wildly different from present-day Israel that you can't pretend it would be the same state as the one we see now. It would entail such a radically dramatic overhaul of Israeli civilization, such a comprehensive dismantling of deeply ingrained racism, such a drastic restructuring of governmental and living systems, so much labor, sacrifice, humility, inner work and reparations, that to call it by the same name as the state that presently exists would be nonsensical.

And that isn't what the liberals in question are talking about instituting when they say they oppose Israel's

atrocities in Gaza but "support Israel's right to exist". What they are saying is they want Israel to remain the unjust and tyrannical apartheid state that is has always been, but for the killing to stop. They want the injustice to continue, but they want its most overt manifestations to stop causing them cognitive dissonance. They want the status quo, without the murderous savagery that is necessary for the status quo's existence. They want to pretend they live in an imaginary fantasyland where such a thing is possible.

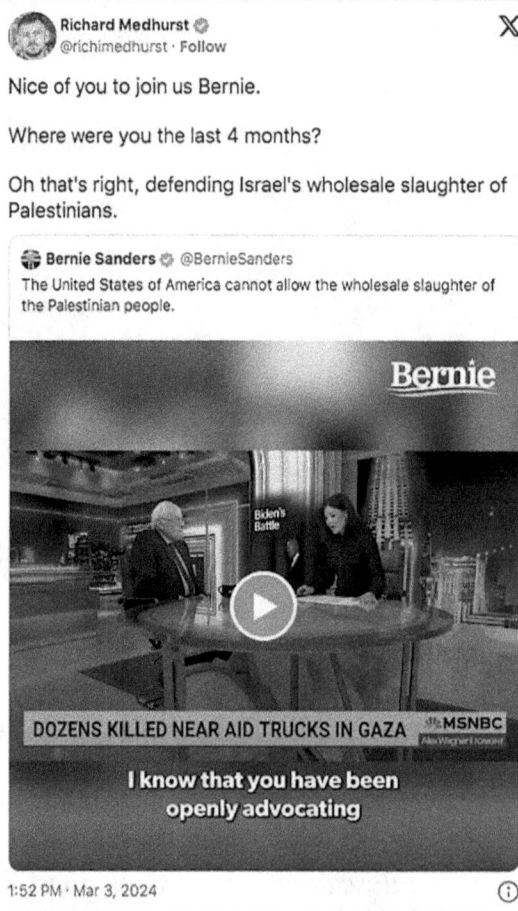

In order to make this fantasy seem more believable, liberals will pretend that the violence we are seeing can be blamed entirely on the Netanyahu government, as though things would be fine without Bibi in office despite the fact that Israel's abusiveness began long before he showed up, and despite the fact that Israel's atrocities in Gaza have the approval of the vast majority of Israelis.

Israeli violence isn't the product of Netanyahu, Netanyahu is the product of Israeli violence. He built his political career upon sentiments that were already in place.

They'll also tell themselves fairy tales about a two-state solution to make their position seem more valid, ignoring inconvenient facts like that Israeli officials have been openly saying a Palestinian state will never happen, that Israeli Jews overwhelmingly oppose such a measure, and that Israeli settlements are being built in Palestinian territories with the explicit goal of making a future two-state solution impossible. Liberals subscribe to these fantasies as a kind of cognitive pacifier, which allows them to relax and feel okay with themselves despite the fact that they're not actually endorsing any viable path toward justice.

And to be clear this isn't just what liberals do with regard to Israel-Palestine; it's their whole entire position on everything. On every issue their position is little more than "Maintain the status quo, but make it pretty and psychologically comfortable for me." They never want to do what's right, they just want to feel like they are right. Theirs is an imperialist, militarist, tyrannical oligarchic ideology with a bunch of feel-good social justice bumper stickers slapped on top of it. A boot on your neck and a flower in its hair.

That's who liberals are. It's who they've always been. Phil Ochs released the song "Love Me, I'm a Liberal" in 1966, and they haven't changed one iota ever since. The issues change, their arguments change, but their "maintain the status quo but let me feel nice about it" values system has remained exactly the same for generations.

Featured image via Gage Skidmore (CC BY-SA 2.0)

Haaretz.com ✓
@haaretzcom · Follow

X

In an effort to avoid harming soldiers and dogs, the IDF has been experimenting with the use of robots and remote-controlled dogs in the Gaza War

So They're Experimenting With Military Robots In Gaza Now

One of the most horrifying facts about this dystopia we live in is that large-scale military operations are routinely used as testing grounds for new war machinery, using human bodies as guinea pigs for experimentation in what amount to giant blood-soaked field laboratories—all to benefit the strategic objectives of empire managers and the profit margins of the military-industrial complex.

Haaretz has a new article out titled "Gaza Becomes Israel's Testing Ground for Military Robots", which reports that "In an effort to avoid harming soldiers and dogs, the IDF has been experimenting with the use of robots and remote-controlled dogs in the Gaza War."

(Yeah because my gosh, can you imagine how terrible it would be if Israeli soldiers and dogs got harmed while carrying out a genocide?)

The article's author Sagi Cohen reports that drone-mounted robot dogs and remotely controlled bulldozers are two of the new apocalyptic horrors currently being battle-tested in Gaza, saying "defense establishment officials confirm that there has been a leap in the use and sophistication of robots on the battlefield." Which is a pretty disconcerting sentence to read.

This news comes out at the same time as a new Public Citizen report warning of the likely imminent arrival of autonomous weapons systems which will kill people with minimal instruction from human pilots, saying "The most serious worry involving autonomous weapons is that they inherently dehumanize the people targeted and make it easier to tolerate widespread killing, including in violation of international human rights law."

The more normalized robots become within the world's militaries the closer we come to this point, and steps are already being taken in that direction. As Common Dreams' Thor Benson notes in an article about the Public Citizen report, "Israel has purchased and at times deployed self-piloting, lethal drones."

Back in January I wrote that "Gaza is a live laboratory for the military industrial complex," saying "Data is with absolute certainty being collected on all the newer weapons being field-tested on human bodies in Gaza (just like has been happening in Ukraine) to be used to benefit the war machine and arms industry."

What sparked this comment at the time was reports and first-hand witness accounts we'd seen coming out about the prolific use of IDF "sniper drones" in Gaza since October, with Israeli forces frequently shooting Palestinians with quad drones armed with rifles. Copious records are most assuredly being compiled on the effectiveness of these newer weapons and tactics in ending human lives, which will then be used to help market those weapons to other states and to improve their efficiency in killing.

When I say this is most assuredly happening, I am not being hyperbolic for effect. Author and journalist Antony Loewenstein gave a lengthy interview on The Chris Hedges Report back in December about Israel's long and extensively documented history of using Gaza as a testing ground for new weapons, spyware, surveillance and security systems, AI, drones, and tactics, which has profited scores of corporations and enabled Israel to become a player of outsized success in the global weapons industry.

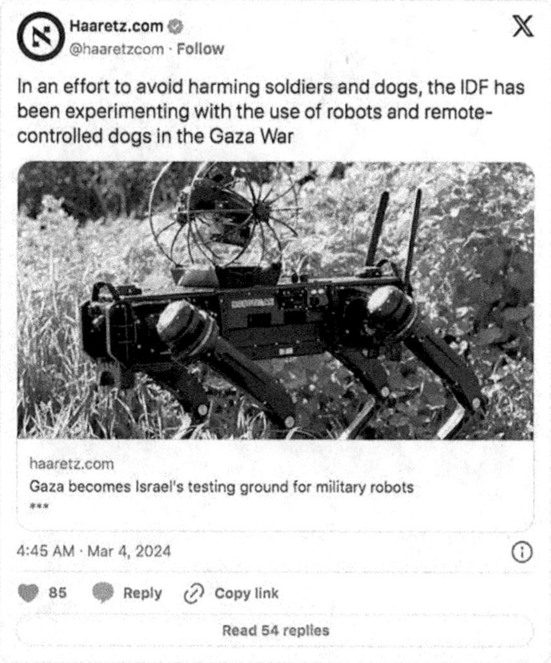

Haaretz.com
@haaretzcom · Follow

In an effort to avoid harming soldiers and dogs, the IDF has been experimenting with the use of robots and remote-controlled dogs in the Gaza War

haaretz.com
Gaza becomes Israel's testing ground for military robots
***

4:45 AM · Mar 4, 2024

85   Reply   Copy link

Read 54 replies

"Israel's drones, surveillance technology including spyware, facial recognition software, and biometric gathering infrastructure, along with smart fences, experimental bombs, and AI-controlled machine guns are all tried out on the captive population in Gaza, often with lethal results," says Hedges in introduction. "These weapons and technologies are then certified as 'battle-tested' and sold around the world."

This doesn't only happen in Gaza. This past September The Wall Street Journal published an article titled "The War in Ukraine Is Also a Giant Arms Fair," subtitled "Arms makers are getting orders for weapons being put to the test on the battlefield." In January of last year CNN published a report titled "How Ukraine became a testbed for Western weapons and battlefield innovation," with one source saying that Ukraine is "absolutely a weapons lab in every sense because none of this equipment has ever actually been used in a war between two industrially developed nations."

And of course we are also seeing this same phenomenon in Africa. In 2021 Mintpress News published a report by Scott Timcke titled "West Africa is the Latest Testing Ground for US Military Artificial Intelligence" about this very same trend. In 2020 Libya saw what is believed to have been the first time a human being has ever been killed by a fully automated drone attack—that is, killed without the machine having been told to do so by a human.

The other day we discussed how the empire's great weakness is that it depends on normal human beings to carry out its orders and turn the gears of the machine. If you look at the facts and think about them for a moment, it's not hard to see how the empire managers are hoping to overcome this weakness in the future.

Nobody With Real Power Cares If You Refuse To Vote For Biden

There's been a lot of talk in pro-Palestine circles about withholding votes for Biden in protest of his genocide in Gaza, which is of course fine, but the discourse around doing so often misses an important point. A lot of US voters erroneously think they'd be punishing the Democrats for Gaza by costing them the election, mistakenly assuming Democrats care about winning. They don't.

Losing an election costs Democratic party leaders nothing; all the career politicians and political operatives at the top keep their careers either way. From their point of view this is just a cushy job with sweet benefits, and they keep those win or lose. And obviously Biden himself doesn't care; he'll have a comfortable retirement regardless of the outcome in November, and on some level he's surely aware that it's nuts for a dementia patient to be in the White House anyway.

If the Democrats cared about getting your vote they'd be trying hard to earn it. They're not trying because they don't care.

The unelected empire managers who actually run the US power structure also don't care who wins the election. They know they'll still get their murder and militarism and capitalism and imperialism no matter who gets sworn in next year, whether it's Biden or Trump or Harris or someone else. Nobody with any real power cares about your vote.

And that's the real issue. That's the real point that keeps getting missed here. The problem is not that the wrong people keep getting elected, it's that the elections don't matter and voters don't have a say. It's that humanity is dominated by a murderous globe-spanning power structure loosely centralized around Washington whose actual movements and behavior have effectively zero responsiveness to the will of the electorate.

You're never going to be able to vote your way out of this mess, and you're never going to be able to not-vote your way out of this mess, because the power of your vote has been undermined to a value of zero. That doesn't mean there's no way out of this mess, it just means there's no way to get out of this mess using the fake plastic diversion toy they handed you to shut you up and trick you into thinking you have a say.

There are still plenty of other tools in the toolbox for forcing an evil power structure to stop doing evil things, but they require a whole lot of hands to bring about, and right now we don't have them. Too many people have been successfully propagandized into believing the status quo works and their government is basically good, or successfully manipulated into giving up on politics altogether and throwing their attention into other things.

Before the people can begin using the power of their numbers to force real change, they're going to have to be awakened to the reality that everything they've been told about their government, their society and their world is a lie. They've got to come to the understanding that the mainstream news media are nothing but propaganda and they live under the most murderous and tyrannical regime on this planet. They've got to realize that this power structure does not ultimately serve their interests, or the interests of their fellow human beings around the world. Only when enough eyes open to this reality can revolutionary change via direct action become possible.

The good news is it's entirely possible to help get those eyes open. Everything you do to help share the truth with your fellow citizens and spread awareness of what's really going on pushes this possibility toward reality. The more people open their eyes, the more people there are to help open others, so this could snowball from impossible to probable to inevitable quite quickly.

An entire globe-spanning empire rests on a closed pair of eyelids. Once they snap open, the whole thing will crumble. And from there we can begin building a healthy world together.

Featured image via Adobe Stock.

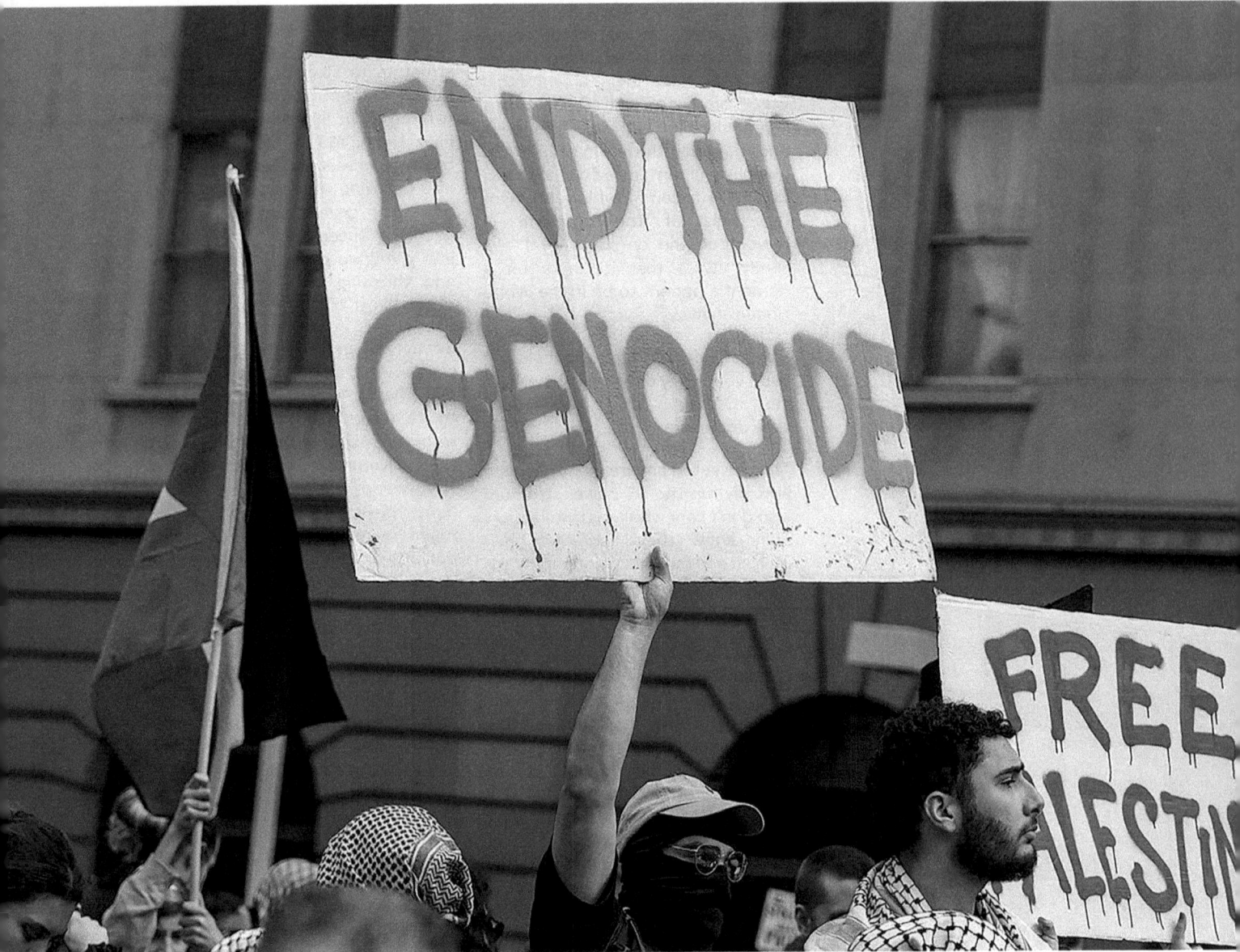

"Pay No Attention To That Genocide Right In Front Of Your Face"

"Pay no attention to that genocide right in front of your face."

That's the constant message we're getting from the dominant institutions in this present-day dystopia. From our news media. From our political parties. From our government. From our mainstream culture of diversion and superficiality.

"Pay no attention to that genocide right in front of your face."

We can see it happening. It's right there. And they know we can see it happening. But they're telling us to ignore it anyway. Pay attention to this other far less urgent news story instead. Pay attention to what a big meany Donald Trump is. Pay attention to Hamas and October 7 2023. Pay attention to this trend, this TV show, this funny video, this celebrity, this product, this event. Pay attention to anything other than the horror you can see unfolding with your own two eyes right this very moment.

"Pay no attention to that genocide right in front of your face."

And most are obeying this command. Society's still puttering along like everything's fine and normal. The shows, events, social engagements and small talk is all still happening in more or less the same way it was happening on October 6 2023. Attention is going everywhere but to the screaming, hemorrhaging elephant in the room.

"Pay no attention to that genocide right in front of your face."

It's an insult to our intelligence. It's an insult to our hearts. It's an insult to our humanity. They're sticking their long, rapey fingers into our minds and commanding us to twist and turn our attention in every direction except where it is most urgently needed, and most of us are submitting to their will and doing as they command. We're putting on a degrading and dehumanizing performance for our rulers to show how far into knots we will contort our minds, our perception and our sense of reality for their convenience.

"Pay no attention to that genocide right in front of your face."

Refusing to obey this command is a daily act of defiance. It's an act of protest each and every moment we refuse to acquiesce to this demand. In each instant we hold our gaze on Gaza and remind others to do the same, we are defying the orders of our rulers. We are disobeying the instructions from the propaganda machine. We are being directly insubordinate to our politicians and our government, and we are disrespecting the plastic smileyface dystopia they supervise.

"Pay no attention to that genocide right in front of your face."

Yeah I'm gonna keep paying attention to that genocide, actually, and I'm going to keep working to get others to do the same. No matter how much you try to turn my gaze away. No matter how ugly your atrocities become. No matter what names you call me or what accusations you level at me. It's right there. We can all see it. I refuse to play along with this demented charade. Israel is committing genocide, our western governments are helping them, the sky is blue, a spade's a spade, and the emperor has no clothes.

Featured image via Matt Hrkac (CC BY 2.0)

The Difference Between Republicans And Democrats

The difference between Republicans and Democrats is that if a Republican president were to back a genocide it would be an evil and unforgivable atrocity, whereas when a Democrat president backs a genocide it's a minor foible that you'd better shut up about unless you want Trump to win.

The difference between Republicans and Democrats is that Republicans want to keep destroying Gaza because they love killing Muslims, whereas Democrats want to keep destroying Gaza because something something it's all Netanyahu's fault anyway hey let's go back to talking about Trump.

The difference between Republicans and Democrats is that Republicans argue in support of wars, militarism, capitalism and oppression using right-wing language, whereas Democrats argue in support of wars, militarism, capitalism and oppression using left-wing language.

The difference between Republicans and Democrats is that Republicans do evil things for evil reasons, whereas Democrats do evil things for noble humanitarian reasons.

The difference between Republicans and Democrats is that Republicans facilitate all the interests of the US empire because America is strong and godly and should rule the world, whereas Democrats facilitate all the interests of the US empire because America is liberal and egalitarian and defends the rules-based international order.

The difference between Republicans and Democrats is that Republicans want to start a world war with China, whereas Democrats are strongly in favor of starting a world war with Russia.

The difference between Republicans and Democrats is that Republicans cheered for the invasion of Iraq solely because it was waged by George W Bush, whereas Democrats criticized the invasion of Iraq solely because it was waged by George W Bush.

The difference between Republicans and Democrats is that the people massacring civilians in the global south under Republican administrations are racist homophobic misogynistic bigots, whereas the people massacring civilians in the global south under Democratic administrations are inclusive intersectional feminist LGBTQ allies.

The difference between Republicans and Democrats is that Republicans criticize Democrats for made-up nonsense reasons like wokeness, whereas Democrats criticize Republicans for made-up nonsense reasons like Russiagate.

The difference between Republicans and Democrats is that Republicans promise to end civil rights if you vote Republican, whereas Democrats promise to let Republicans end civil rights if you vote Republican.

The difference between Republicans and Democrats is that Republicans are led by demented octogenarian swamp monsters who can't string a sentence together and have spent decades in office promoting ecocide, imperialism, exploitation and oligarchy, whereas Democrats—oh, well I guess that one's both of them actually.

The difference between Republicans and Democrats is that liberals feel bad feelings when Republicans are overseeing the imperial bloodbaths and feel good feelings when Democrats are.

The difference between Republicans and Democrats is that when a Republican is president it's time to yell and scream about any bad things he does, whereas when a Democrat is president it's time for brunch.

The difference between Republicans and Democrats is that when Republicans do the monstrous things necessary to maintain a globe-spanning empire they're the greater evil, whereas when Democrats do the monstrous things necessary to maintain a globe-spanning empire they're the lesser evil.

The difference between Republicans and Democrats is that when the imperial murder machine has an (R) on it we're meant to frown, and when the imperial murder machine has a (D) on it we're meant to smile.

You Can't Be A "Lesser Evil" When You're Sponsoring A Genocide

You don't get to apply the label "lesser evil" to a president who is backing a literal genocide. That's not a thing. Past a certain point you're just plain evil.

If you were to make a list of the absolute worst things a powerful leader can do, genocide and carelessness with nuclear brinkmanship should be on the very top of that list. Biden has done both of these. You can't legitimately call such a person a "lesser evil".

•

Israel supporters are scum. Lower than them are the Biden supporters who avoid thinking too hard about his genocide in Gaza and make excuses for it, because at least the Israel supporters are honest about what they are. Lower even than the overt Bidenists are the "progressives" who condemn Israel's actions out of one side of their mouths while still pushing the need to vote for Biden out the other, because they're even less honest about themselves than the outright shitlibs. If you're going to be a genocidal shitstain, at least do it without also sowing confusion and muddying the waters.

•

So it turns out The New York Times hired an actual genocide supporter who'd never even been a reporter before to co-author atrocity propaganda about mass rapes on October 7. If the western media actually told the truth and reported the news, this revelation would be a major international story today.

•

Being an ally country to the USA is like being friends with a really bitchy drama queen where you're only allowed to help her tear down her social enemies and can't ever talk about what she's doing to create all the conflict in her life because if you do she'll come for you next.

•

Palestinian lives are more important than western feelings. It doesn't matter if criticizing Biden's actions makes your feelings feel nervous about Trump. It doesn't matter if pro-Palestine activism makes your feelings feel like you've been persecuted. Your feelings don't matter.

•

X

@zei_squirrel · Follow

oh my god. One of the three authors of the New York Times' "mass rape" atrocity propaganda hoax is Anat Schwartz. She liked posts calling for Gaza to be turned into a "slaughterhouse". This the person the NYT hired to write about Palestinians and frame them as sub-human monsters

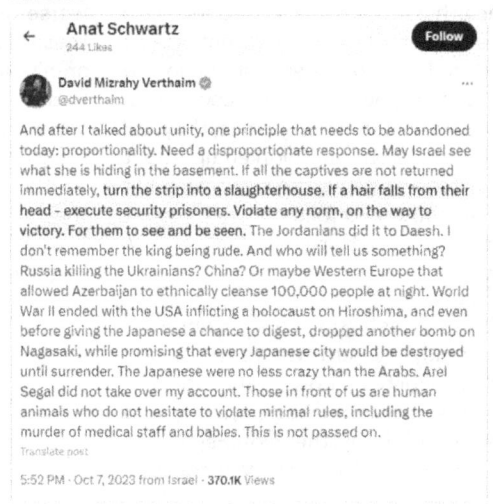

← **Anat Schwartz**   Follow
244 Likes

David Mizrahy Verthaim ✓
@dverthaim

And after I talked about unity, one principle that needs to be abandoned today: proportionality. Need a disproportionate response. May Israel see what she is hiding in the basement. If all the captives are not returned immediately, turn the strip into a slaughterhouse. If a hair falls from their head - execute security prisoners. Violate any norm, on the way to victory. For them to see and be seen. The Jordanians did it to Daesh. I don't remember the king being rude. And who will tell us something? Russia killing the Ukrainians? China? Or maybe Western Europe that allowed Azerbaijan to ethnically cleanse 100,000 people at night. World War II ended with the USA inflicting a holocaust on Hiroshima, and even before giving the Japanese a chance to digest, dropped another bomb on Nagasaki, while promising that every Japanese city would be destroyed until surrender. The Japanese were no less crazy than the Arabs. Arel Segal did not take over my account. Those in front of us are human animals who do not hesitate to violate minimal rules, including the murder of medical staff and babies. This is not passed on.
Translate post

5:52 PM · Oct 7, 2023 from Israel · 370.1K Views

Western liberal leaders are always trying to get you to trade feelings in exchange for concrete improvements in material conditions. Now Biden administration officials are proclaiming how "disappointed" they are in the Netanyahu government for approving thousands of new West Bank settlements, even as they continue their unconditional material support for Israeli butchery of Palestinians. Before that western leaders were all babbling about how "concerned" they are about the impending assault on Rafah while physically pouring more and more weapons into Israel. Before that they were telling everyone we should focus on how some Jewish Zionists feel threatened by pro-Palestine demonstrations instead of focusing on the human butchery that is being experienced by Gazans.

You see this over and over again, on all issues. You want an end to genocide, they solemnly tell you their hearts are with the people of Gaza who are experiencing unimaginable hardship—but never actually do anything to stop it. You want an end to police brutality, they tell you they hear you, they support you, they stand with you—but never actually change policing policy. You want healthcare, they tell you to focus on getting emotionally hysterical about Donald Trump instead of helping to improve your material conditions. You want economic justice, they tell you to instead get worked up about culture war issues the powerful don't care about and focus on how good it feels to be on the correct side of that war.

They've set up this counterfeit currency system where you hand them political power and consent to the murderousness, tyranny and exploitation of the globe-spanning empire—and they pay you for it in feelings.

"Here is unipolar planetary hegemony," we tell them.

"And here are your feelings," they reply magnanimously.

"Here is our consent for unfettered capitalism, neoliberal imperialist extraction, wars, militarism, starvation sanctions and proxy conflicts," we say.

"And as payment for your product, we present you with some feelings," they tell us with a warm smile.

"Here is our health, the health of our biosphere, our future, and our sanity," we say.

"And here's a big fat briefcase full of feelings," they reply.

The message we're fed over and over again is that feelings matter more than Palestinian lives. Feelings matter more than your neighbors having a roof over their head and being able to provide for their children. Feelings matter more than freedom from tyranny and abuse. Feelings matter more than the ecosystem we depend on for survival. Feelings matter more than avoiding nuclear armageddon.

And everything keeps on getting worse and worse, and somehow all these feelings we're being traded aren't actually making us feel any better. Somehow supporting the correct leaders who say the correct words isn't actually improving anything. We've traded these people the entire world, and looked down to find ourselves holding a big plastic bag of Monopoly money.

Featured image via Gage Skidmore (CC BY-SA 2.0)

Israel Supporters Are Some Of The Worst People In The World

Yesterday I shared a tweet about how Doctors Without Borders are now encountering children as young as five in Gaza who say they want to die because of the horrific things they have experienced during Israel's ongoing genocidal onslaught.

It's just about the most awful thing you can imagine, tiny children being so traumatized that they consciously don't want to go on living. It boggles the mind to even contemplate it. But almost as soon as I shared my post, I got a response from an Israel supporter saying, "Gazans support Hamas. Hamas conducts Islamic extremist terror. Gazans should reconsider their support for Hamas."

Later I got another response from an account with a bunch of flag emojis next to its name saying, "Before shedding tears for the people of Gaza, remember that they created Hamas, elected it, supported it, supplied it, worked for it, hid it, sheltered it, filled its ranks and celebrated all its atrocities."

I received another response from an anonymous account saying "FAFO", an acronym for "Fuck Around, Find Out". Used here, it means that those small children who want to die because of the horrors they have experienced actually deserve it, because they are Gazan. Which is also essentially what the other two responders were saying as well.

Imagine being that way. Imagine being so warped and twisted inside that you think that's a sane and appropriate way to respond to unthinkable news about small children being so traumatized by mass military violence that they want to die.

This happens all the time. The other day I shared a report from an American doctor saying that IDF snipers have been picking off Gazan children with single shots to the head, and I again received a comment from someone saying "Fuck around and find out."

They're essentially standing over a pile of child corpses and puffing their chests like a guy who just won a pub brawl.

It might seem kind of petty to focus on individual comments from random social media accounts, but this happens so often, and I see other people talking about it too—I just saw

a screenshot of a guy saying "fuck around and find out" in response to that gut-wrenching photo of a dead Palestinian girl ripped apart by an Israeli airstrike in Rafah earlier this month. So this is definitely a symptom of something profoundly ugly lurking in the underbelly of our society that's worth drawing some attention to.

If you don't interact with many Zionists in your day to day life or don't have a large enough profile to be constantly swarmed by Israel apologists you might be unaware that this is happening, but the vitriol I've been seeing from Israel supporters on social media platforms since October 7 has been one of the most shocking and disturbing things I've ever witnessed.

Every single day these last four and a half months I've been inundated with comments from Israel supporters excusing the most monstrous acts imaginable in the most monstrous ways imaginable. People calling for the total destruction of Gaza. People saying the Gazans deserve what is happening to them. Saying the sickest shit you can possibly think of in response to news of terrible things happening to innocent children.

Over the years I've butted heads with pretty much every political faction in

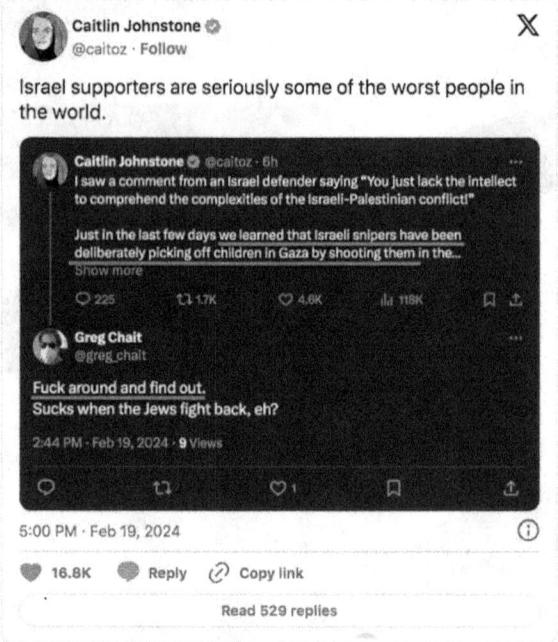

Caitlin Johnstone @caitoz · Follow

Israel supporters are seriously some of the worst people in the world.

> Caitlin Johnstone @caitoz · 6h
> I saw a comment from an Israel defender saying "You just lack the intellect to comprehend the complexities of the Israeli-Palestinian conflict!"
>
> Just in the last few days we learned that Israeli snipers have been deliberately picking off children in Gaza by shooting them in the...
> Show more
>
> 225   1.7K   4.6K   118K
>
> Greg Chait @greg_chait
>
> Fuck around and find out.
> Sucks when the Jews fight back, eh?
>
> 2:44 PM · Feb 19, 2024 · 9 Views
>
> 1

5:00 PM · Feb 19, 2024

16.8K   Reply   Copy link

Read 529 replies

Hadi Nasrallah @HadiNasrallah

There is something really demonic about zionists.

> Muhammad Smiry @Muham... · 1h
> From Rafah this night
>
> 0:13
>
> From مصطفى محمود
>
> 108   2.4K   3.1K   192K
>
> Avi Denovitz @TheCousinAvi · 57m
> Fuck around and find out 😈
>
> 9   2   1.1K

2:20 PM · Feb 12, 2024 · 1.6M Views

1K   24K   90K   1.2K

the English-speaking world at one point or another, and I can honestly say that Israel supporters are by far the absolute worst. No political faction I have ever interacted with is as immoral and dishonest, or so frequently says things that are so jaw-droppingly disgusting I am sure I must be misinterpreting it at first. I've never tangled with a more odious group of people.

And to be clear I'm not talking about a faction of just Israelis or Jews here; a huge percentage of these awful comments come from Christian Zionists and American rightists, with a decent smattering of Hindu nationalists from India who'll support any excuse to cheerlead the killing of Muslims. The only unifying feature I'm seeing in the faction I'm talking about is that they support Israel and its actions in Gaza. What I'm saying here will be spun as antisemitic by Israel supporters no matter how I put it because Israel supporters are manipulative liars, but to be clear this is not about Jews at all.

There's something seriously, seriously wrong with these people. They have no interest in truth or morality; all they care about is supporting their favorite ethnostate and murdering Palestinians. I guess when you're

---

an actual goblin
@gobloid3 · Follow   X

when israel supporters say stuff like "what did hamas expect" and "fuck around and find out" this is all i hear

Helmut Kämpfe (31 July 1909 – 10 June 1944) was a Waffen SS *Sturmbannführer* who was captured and executed by the French Resistance. In retribution, the Germans carried out the Oradour massacre in occupied France on 10 June 1944. In total 643 men, women and children were killed in Oradour-sur-Glane by troops from the 2nd SS Panzer Division *Das Reich*. The SS commander who ordered the massacre said the death of Kämpfe was the reason for the killings.

3:05 PM · Nov 24, 2023   ⓘ

♥ 4.1K   Reply   ⌁ Copy link

Read 18 replies

---

already able to numb your heart and your mind enough to support an apartheid state that whose existence requires nonstop violence and abuse, when that state ramps up its atrocities to historic levels you're not going to have enough of a conscience to see anything wrong with it.

Anyway that's my rant for today. Just had to get that out. I don't know what to do about any of this, but it's probably worth bringing some consciousness to.

Featured image via Adobe Stock.

On Aaron Bushnell, Methinks The Israel Apologist Doth Protest Too Much

Currently there has been a famine going on for months in a place that is half children, which means that in the coming days we can expect a massive explosion of children dying due to starvation. And here's the kicker: the famine is 100 percent deliberate.

I never thought I'd ever see anything worse than babies being ripped apart by military explosives until I started seeing babies being starved. Babies killed with bombs is horrifying, but starving babies causes PANIC. It triggers a deep, primal THIS NEEDS TO STOP instinct.

•

Aaron Bushnell wasn't addressing the Israeli government with his soul-jarring message. He wasn't even addressing his own government. He was addressing you. Each of us. His goal was to get us all to open our eyes to the horror of what's happening, and spur us to action to end it.

•

If you've noticed Israel apologist trolls swarming all over the Aaron Bushnell story, it's because they know how damaging a US airman self-immolating while screaming "Free Palestine" is to US and Israeli information interests, and they're scrambling to manipulate the narrative.

Israel apologists are all over the internet swarming the comments of anyone discussing Aaron Bushnell going "No one cares! He died for nothing! He didn't accomplish anything!" Bitch if he didn't accomplish anything you wouldn't be here in my notifications frantically telling me he didn't accomplish anything.

Who do these losers think they're kidding? The very fact that they need to do this proves them wrong. They're like a guy who spends hours sending a woman dozens of texts about how he totally doesn't care that she rejected his advances. Methinks the Israel apologist doth protest too much.

•

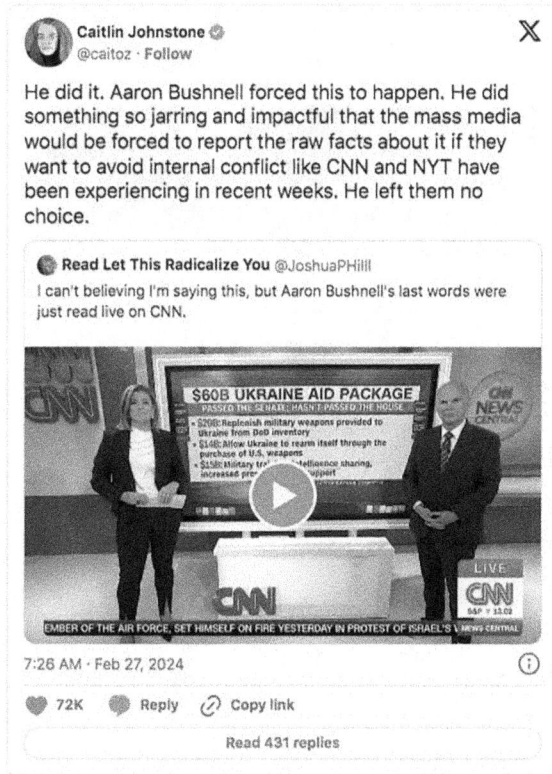

Caitlin Johnstone ✓
@caitoz · Follow

He did it. Aaron Bushnell forced this to happen. He did something so jarring and impactful that the mass media would be forced to report the raw facts about it if they want to avoid internal conflict like CNN and NYT have been experiencing in recent weeks. He left them no choice.

Read Let This Radicalize You @JoshuaPHilll
I can't believing I'm saying this, but Aaron Bushnell's last words were just read live on CNN.

7:26 AM · Feb 27, 2024

♥ 72K   Reply   Copy link

Read 431 replies

Many high-profile Israel supporters have been circulating a fake screenshot of a Reddit account run by Bushnell saying "Palestine will be free when all the jews are dead." The fact that they're doing this illustrates two things: that Israel supporters are unscrupulous liars, and that they are freaking the fuck out about how much damage Bushnell has done to their cause.

•

Israel supporters keep confidently opining on Aaron Bushnell's motives and character as though they are even remotely capable of understanding such a person. These weak, shallow, self-centered little bitches can't even lay siege to Gaza without bringing along cotton candy machines and bouncy castles.

•

Liberals: We support the fight for civil rights!

*Palestine supporters: *boycott**

Liberals: No not like that.

*Palestine supporters: *protest**

Liberals: No not like that.

*Palestinians: *violent resistance**

Liberals: No not like that.

*Aaron Bushnell: *sets self on fire**

Liberals: No not like that.

•

US liberals in 2016: Wanting universal healthcare is a pie in the sky fantasy
US liberals in 2020: Wanting full student loan debt forgiveness is a pie in the sky fantasy
US liberals in 2024: Wanting your country not to commit genocide is a pie in the sky fantasy

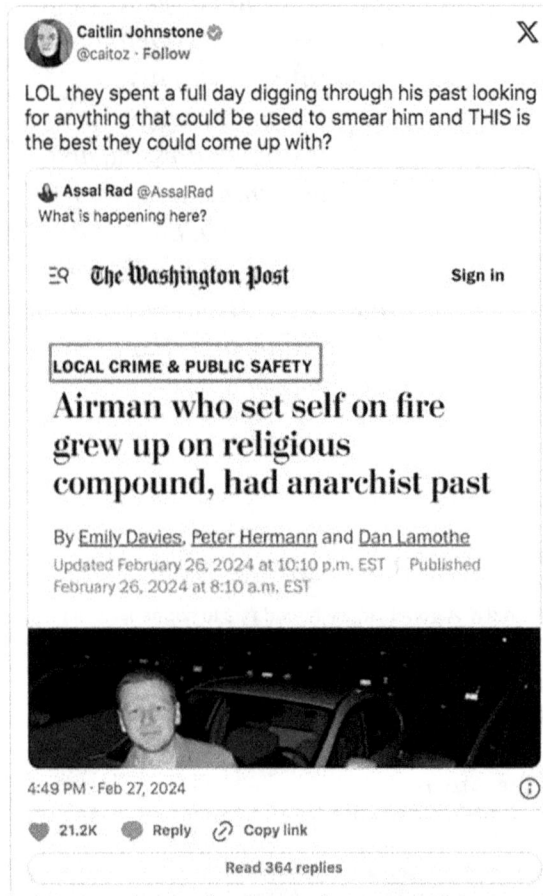

•

Caitlin Johnstone @caitoz · Follow

LOL they spent a full day digging through his past looking for anything that could be used to smear him and THIS is the best they could come up with?

Assal Rad @AssalRad
What is happening here?

The Washington Post   Sign in

LOCAL CRIME & PUBLIC SAFETY

Airman who set self on fire grew up on religious compound, had anarchist past

By Emily Davies, Peter Hermann and Dan Lamothe

Updated February 26, 2024 at 10:10 p.m. EST | Published February 26, 2024 at 8:10 a.m. EST

4:49 PM · Feb 27, 2024

21.2K   Reply   Copy link

Read 364 replies

If the United States really was the defender of justice it purports to be and actually used its military in the way it claims to, it would have told Israel to cease its genocidal atrocities in Gaza and taken military action if Israel refused. Instead, it's actively running support for Israel's atrocities.

This shows you what the US empire really is, and what it has always been. This shows you that its "humanitarian interventions" have never actually had humanitarian goals. It shows you that every time the US has attacked a foreign nation under the narrative cover of freeing its people from its tyrannical government was in fact an act of mass military violence based on lies.

There's nothing stopping the US from moving its war machinery to the immediate surroundings of Israel and threatening to destroy IDF locations if it doesn't cease its massacres, in the same way Hugh Thompson and his helicopter crew rightly stopped the My Lai massacre by threatening to fire on US troops in Vietnam. That hasn't happened because the US isn't what it pretends to be, and does not use its military in the way it claims to.

In reality, the US is the hub of a globe-spanning power structure that requires endless violence to maintain its hegemony, and what we're seeing in Gaza is just one more expression of that violence. This isn't some fluke aberration in the US empire's behavior but a very normal and expected manifestation of it. The facts clash with the United States' story about itself because the story is a lie.

•

Ralph Nader has an article out arguing that the real death count from Israel's onslaught in Gaza is probably at least 200,000. This could very well be true; it is definitely suspect how the official death count has been hovering around 30,000 for weeks while we know people are being deliberately starved at an incredibly fast pace and the massacres haven't stopped. We've seen severe death count lags before in places like Yemen, where in 2017 the media stopped counting at 10,000 deaths and just kept repeating that number for ages.

•

Every Hollywood celebrity who fails to speak out against the US-backed genocide in Gaza at the Academy Awards this Sunday is complicit in that genocide. If you're given a major platform and your government is committing genocide, you are morally obligated use that platform to condemn your government's actions.

•

I always get Israel supporters in my comments going "Hurr hurr, if you think what Aaron Bushnell did is so great then why don't you do it too?"

I am not brave enough or selfless enough to follow Aaron Bushnell's example. No one is; that's why what he did is having such a massive impact, and it's why Israel supporters have been freaking out about him ever since. It was a superhuman act of protest.

Shallow, vapid people are incapable of understanding and appreciating what Aaron Bushnell did. They've no internal framework for it. When they dismiss him or disparage his motives, they're just telling you there's not much to them as people. They're asleep at the wheel of life.

•

A political party which views opposing an active genocide as a fringe extremist position is not a political party that should continue to exist.

•

After seeing how horrifyingly murderous and reckless this Democrat president has turned out to be, I hope US leftists have fully let go of all the guilt liberals tried to heap on them for not rallying behind the Democrat in 2016. It was all a lie. They're as bad as Republicans.

•

Over and over you see people enter western mainstream political parties with the stated goal of changing them from this inside, but instead it changes them. They think the problem is that the party just doesn't have enough nice people in it, but it turns out trying to change a mainstream political party in the western empire by putting nice people in it is like trying to change an abusive cult by putting nice people in it: the cult doesn't change, the people who go in just get indoctrinated. The cult isn't bad because there aren't enough nice cult members, the cult is bad because its entire purpose, function and founding doctrine is bad.

A mainstream political party in the imperial core exists solely to promote the interests of the empire. Everything in it is geared toward this purpose. That is its nature. If you join it, you either embrace its doctrines and help it act out its foundational purpose, or you get kicked out of the cult. You cannot change it. It can only change you. How many times does this have to happen before people learn the lesson?

•

The western-backed genocide in Gaza should be showing everyone that western governments don't make the odd-looking foreign policy decisions they make because they understand foreign policy better than ordinary people. They make those decisions because they are corrupt and evil.

That's always been the case, it's just far more obvious now. You can see just by looking at how universal support for Israel is among US officials and lawmakers compared to the general public that any random schmoe off the street is more likely to make correct and moral foreign policy decisions on behalf of these governments than the empire managers in charge.

And that's why real democracy is continually subverted in those nations. If the people were actually in charge of the foreign policy decisions made within the imperial core, the empire would no longer be inflicting the violence and tyranny necessary for its continued existence.

•

A whole media industry is sprouting up around mainstream journalists just reading The Grayzone and presenting its findings as their own original reporting, because The Grayzone is considered naughty enough to steal from.

•

At this point I just automatically assume that any Israel supporter who interacts with me is acting in bad faith, partly because that's been my consistent experience with them and partly because in order to still support Israel in March of 2024 you have to be a bit sociopathic.

•

Most of the Americans who'll call you an antisemite for criticizing Israel would have mocked you and laughed at you if you called them racist for criticizing Obama or sexist for criticizing Hillary Clinton. It's the exact same logic, but it's okay when they do it.

•

After watching a pro-Palestine activist go off the deep end recently I think it's probably a good idea to issue a few basic reminders to anyone who's speaking out about this issue:

Don't deny the Holocaust unless you want to help delegitimize the pro-Palestine movement. Don't try to make Israeli atrocities about Judaism or Jewishness unless you want to help delegitimize the pro-Palestine movement. Don't conflate Jews as a global collective with a murderous apartheid state unless you want to help delegitimize the pro-Palestine movement. Don't say Jews rule the world unless you want to help delegitimize the pro-Palestine movement.

It's not hard to make these distinctions, and the overwhelming majority of pro-Palestine voices have no difficulty doing so. It's also not hard to see what messages Israel apologists will forcefully amplify as evidence that the entire pro-Palestine movement is antisemitic and that everyone needs to shift the focus from stopping an active genocide to fighting an imaginary antisemitism crisis.

This isn't about Jews, it's about settler-colonialism and the geostrategic objectives of the western empire—both of which we've seen manifest in countless examples that have nothing to do with Jewish people. Zionism is just one belief system the empire managers will utilize to advance their agendas of planetary hegemony, just as they do with Christian fundamentalism, Islamophobia, humanitarianism, conservatism, progressivism, and any other worldview that can be exploited to their advantage.

In short, don't let your opposition to Israeli atrocities turn you into a moron. Don't let your support for the Palestinians turn you into a tool of the empire. Stay on top of that shit. Please and thank you.

Featured image via Adobe Stock.

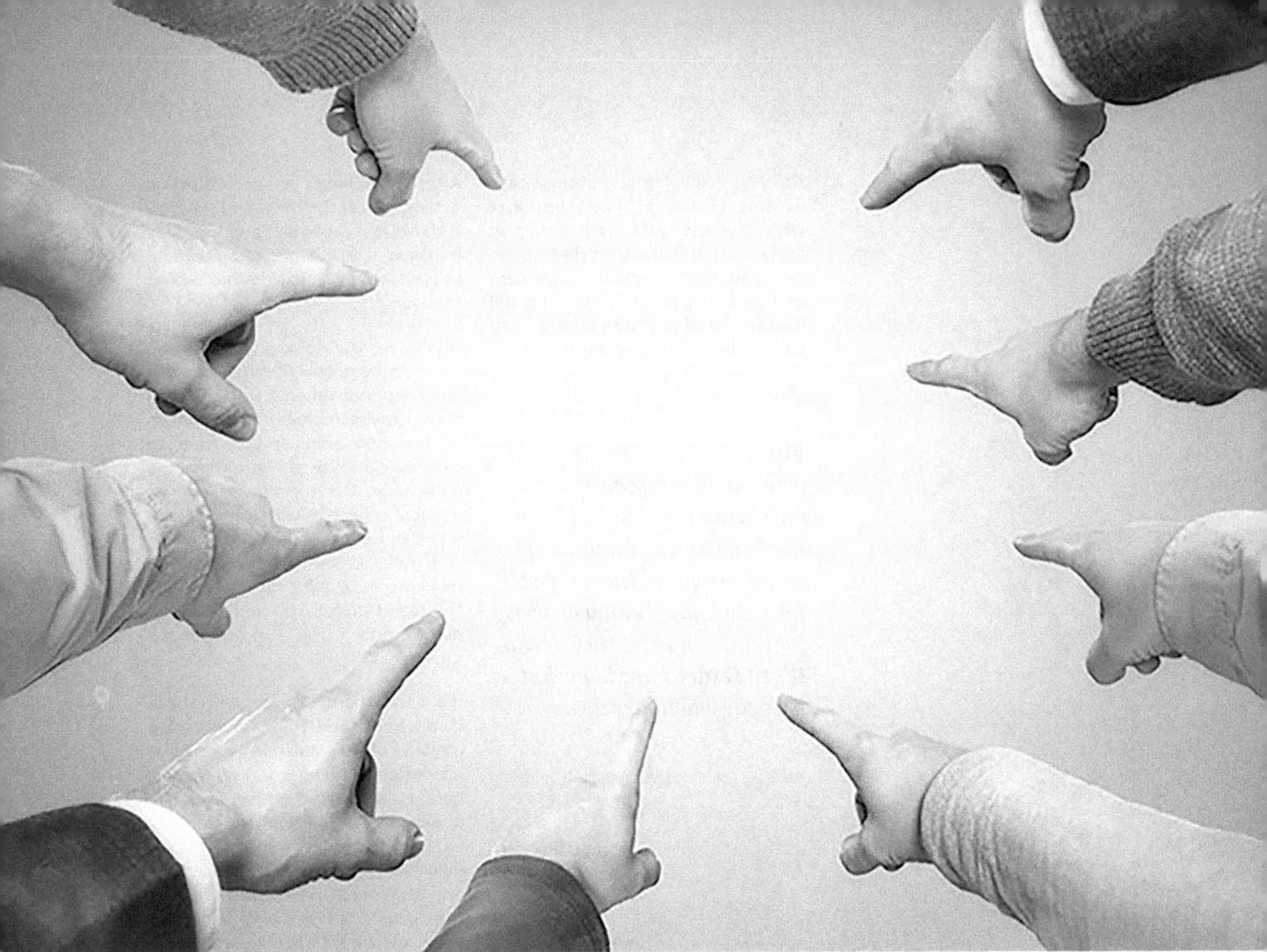

Just Keep Bringing Awareness To The Depravity Of The Empire In As Many Ways As Possible

At this point in history the most effective way for westerners to fight the empire and build support for revolutionary change is to undermine public support for western status quo systems and institutions. One does this by using every means at their disposal to help people see that the power structures which rule over us don't serve our interests, and that they are in fact profoundly evil and destructive.

It takes a flash of insight for a westerner to be able to really see the perniciousness of the US-centralized empire in all its blood-soaked glory. This is because westerners spend their entire lives marinating in empire propaganda from childhood, which has normalized and manufactured their consent for the murderous, exploitative and oppressive power structure we live under. The current status quo is all they've ever known, and the idea that something better might be possible is alien to them.

Teachers of spiritual enlightenment point students to the truth of their being in as many ways as possible in an effort to facilitate a flash of insight into reality. The reason they do that rather than saying the same words over and over again from day to day is because everyone's mind is unique and ever-changing, and what knocks things home for one student one day will just be useless noise to another student who will later pop open at something completely different. The receptivity to insight varies from person to person.

Similarly, a westerner who's been swimming in empire propaganda their whole life won't have their moment of insight into the depraved nature of the empire until something lands for them that they are personally receptive to. Someone who isn't receptive to words about the exploitative and ecocidal nature of global capitalism may be receptive to the threat of rapidly expanding censorship, surveillance, police militarization and other authoritarian measures. Someone who is unbothered by the empire's nuclear brinkmanship with Russia and looming war with China may have their heart broken and their worldview changed when shown what is happening in Gaza.

What triggers the opening of one pair of eyes may not be what triggers another. A kickboxer doesn't throw only overhand rights because that happened to be what scored a knockout in his last bout, he throws a diverse array of strikes in varied combinations at all levels to overwhelm the defenses of his opponent and land a fight-ending blow. When fighting the empire, one needs to bring the same approach.

Look for fresh opportunities to show westerners that the mass media are deceiving and propagandizing them to get them questioning their assumptions about what they've been told about the world. Look for fresh opportunities to show them evidence that the US war machine is the most murderous and destructive force on this planet. Look for fresh opportunities to show them how status quo systems create a far less beneficial society and a far less healthy world than what we could have under different systems. You never know what could be the one thing that snaps somebody's eyes open.

Nothing you do on this front is wasted effort. All positive changes in human behavior at any level are always preceded by an expansion of awareness, so anything you can do to help bring awareness to the reality of our situation is energy well spent. Any effort you make to shove human consciousness toward the light of truth in even the tiniest way has a beneficial effect on our species.

So use whatever tools you can to make that happen. Have conversations, attend demonstrations, put up signs and stickers, write, tweet, make podcasts, make videos—whatever you find effective for you. Just make sure you're coming at this thing from as many angles as possible, because diversifying your attacks on the mind control machine is the best way to get through its defenses.

Featured image via Adobe Stock.

When The Slaughter Stops In Gaza

When the slaughter stops in Gaza
I will get to those cobwebs, promise,
and water that monstera,
and clean out that goo in the fridge.

When the slaughter stops in Gaza
I will youtube how to grow strawberries,
and whether dinosaurs ever had feathers,
and what's the deal with hibachis—
is it something to do with fondue?

When the slaughter stops in Gaza
I will brush my hair out finally,
and call my Mum god bless her
and make her a perfect lasagna—
no, two; I'll make one for freezing,
and I'll give Dad back his drill.

When the slaughter stops in Gaza
I will teach myself 'Nightswimming',
and do a drawing of that face
that I took a pic of with my camera
in that packed tram in peak-hour
Back Before All This Happened,
and I'll make some kind of cake.

When the slaughter stops in Gaza
I will sit with my love in our camp chairs,
our fingers entwined with our heart strings,
kicking coals awake til magpies
chortle "oh boy are you guys still up?"
and then I'll let him give me an orgasm—
the kind that rips through veils.

When the slaughter stops in Gaza
I'll have my friend for dinner,
and we can watch her vampire show
and talk about her Dad
who died seven millennia and three lives ago
in September of 2023.
And we will lay upon the couch
our teeth stained black with wine,
and we will giggle about dumb things,
and one of us will fart
and the other will fall off the couch,
and it will be good and kind and sweet,
and not once will we see dead babies
or kids ripped from their mums,
or servicemen lit on fire
screaming "Free Palestine, FREE PALESTINE!"
and have our hearts thump in our mouths,
teeth clacking like a piano,
nails digging into flesh,
because everything is awful
and nothing makes sense,
and those men are so horrible,
and why won't they stop them
and why won't they stop them
and why won't they stop
why won't they stop

But until then, I will roll out of bed,
do a chore and eat a thing,
brush my teeth and drink some water
thump my chest and howl in sorrow
hug my babies, sniff their hair,
and get back in the fight.

•

STATE OF THE UNION

C-SPAN

• Notes From The Edge Of The Narrative Matrix •

Pretending The US Can't Just Drive Aid Into Gaza

The Biden administration is supposedly planning to set up a temporary pier in Gaza to allow for the large-scale shipment of sorely needed goods into the enclave, which reportedly will take weeks to build and will still be subjected to an Israeli checkpoint. This is on top of the widely ridiculed airdrops of pitifully small amounts of aid the US has already been making in this continuing charade where Washington pretends Gaza is surrounded by some kind of unassailable invisible barrier between itself and Israel.

And hell, why not? Why not build a pier. Have they considered digging a giant tunnel to get aid into Gaza as well? Or launching aid into Gaza by building a giant slingshot? Or perhaps they could invent some type of portal gun à la Rick and Morty?

Ooh! Hey! Or what about simply making their fully dependent client state let the aid in, or force them to stop the genocidal onslaught that makes it necessary? As Antiwar's Dave DeCamp rightly notes of the planned pier construction, "The drastic measure is being ordered instead of Biden using the enormous leverage he has over Israel to pressure them to allow in more aid or halt the genocidal campaign."

•

The Grayzone has a new report out featuring leaked slides from a private Israel lobby presentation teaching politicians and prominent figures how to talk about Gaza in ways the public will be receptive to, based on focus group-tested information gathered by Republican political operative Frank Luntz.

Journalist Mark Ames tweeted of the report, "This is an incredible scoop, a direct window into how the genocide-propaganda sausage is made."

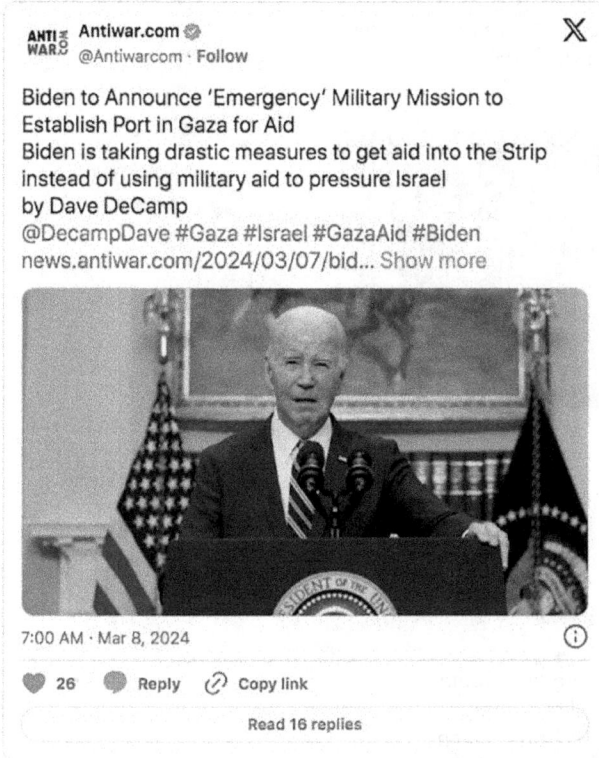

Biden to Announce 'Emergency' Military Mission to Establish Port in Gaza for Aid
Biden is taking drastic measures to get aid into the Strip instead of using military aid to pressure Israel
by Dave DeCamp
@DecampDave #Gaza #Israel #GazaAid #Biden
news.antiwar.com/2024/03/07/bid... Show more

7:00 AM · Mar 8, 2024

26   Reply   Copy link

Read 16 replies

My favorite part of the article is where the author Max Blumenthal writes that Republicans and Democrats were found to be receptive to different words used to describe Israel's genocidal violence in Gaza, saying "Republican voters prefer phrases which imply maximalist violence, like 'eradicate' and 'obliterate,' while sanitized terms like 'neutralize' appeal more to Democrats."

That's pretty much the only difference between Republicans and Democrats right there. That's it in a nutshell.

You see western pundits and politicians criticizing settlements in the West Bank more forcefully than the genocide in Gaza, despite genocide plainly being worse. This is because Israel's approval of West Bank settlements exposes the "two state solution" for the lie that it is and makes it clear that the western power alliance has no meaningful position on Israel's abusive treatment of Palestinians.

When western officials bitch at Israel over settlements, they're essentially saying "Stop it you guys, you're giving the game away! Now how are we supposed to pretend we care?" They need to be able to credibly bleat the phrase "two-state solution" once in a while in order to create the impression that they're not just permanently taking the side of genocide, ethnic cleansing, colonialism, theft and apartheid—even though that is exactly what they are doing.

I've noticed that on social media I'm getting more and more comments from dopey right wingers yelling at me for what I have to say about Gaza, and what's weird is that most of them don't even post about Israel-Palestine normally. They appear to be doing it solely because they see opposition to the Gaza genocide as a left-wing issue, and so they've reflexively taken the opposite position because that's just what political engagement looks like in this insipid, brainwashed dystopia of ours.

Until recently most of the hostile responses I've been getting have been coming from virulent Israel supporters with Israeli flags and "proud Zionist" in their bios who shriek about Hamas 24/7. Now a lot of the pushback I'm getting is just from standard MAGA chuds and other rightists who tweet mostly about partisan politics in their own country. They're not pushing back against me because they love Israel, they're pushing back because I'm a leftist and they automatically push back against lefty-looking things because that's what they've been programmed to do.

It just says so much about the state of western civilization that even genocide has been turned into another vapid culture war wedge issue for people to masturbate their tribal identity constructs on. As though "don't starve children to death or rip them to shreds with military explosives" is some kind of ideological position that only makes sense through a specific political lens, instead of just the normal human default perspective for anyone who isn't a psychopath.

But that's the genius of the empire. Propaganda has been used to split the general population into two warring factions of equal strength, and the propagandists

get each faction arguing about which imperial military project should be supported and which should be criticized. A lot of the people you see supporting the US-backed butchery in Gaza today have spent two years criticizing the US proxy war in Ukraine (and vice versa), because they took those positions based on what the pundits and politicians in their political faction told them to think. It's got nothing to do with values or morals, it's just blind tribalistic herd mentality.

And that's exactly where the empire wants us. Evenly divided against each other too thoroughly to get anything done, arguing back and forth about WHICH imperial agendas should be advanced instead of IF any of them should be advanced. A bunch of bleating human livestock unknowingly bickering about how best to advance the interests of their owners.

Image via CSPAN

• Notes From The Edge Of The Narrative Matrix •

Worrying About TikTok During An Active Genocide

Benjamin Netanyahu says he's going to ignore Biden's "red line" against invading Rafah and launch the planned invasion of the Gaza Strip's southernmost point anyway.

There will surely be grave consequences from Washington for this bold act of defiance, perhaps including Biden saying the words "red line" a second time.

A red line that everyone knows you'll never enforce is not a red line at all; it's just perception management. And Biden has already openly said his "red line" against invading won't be enforced, telling MSNBC "It is a red line, but I am never going to leave Israel. The defense of Israel is still critical. So there is no red line I am going to cut off all weapons, so they don't have the Iron Dome to protect them."

•

Leaked bodycam footage obtained by Al Jazeera reportedly shows a November IDF raid in Gaza in which Israeli troops executed a Palestinian civilian and then laughed and congratulated each other about it afterward.

There's only so much footage you can watch of IDF soldiers gleefully behaving like monsters before you have to admit there's something deeply and profoundly sick about Israeli society itself.

•

The US is playing an imaginary game of The Floor Is Lava by pretending it can't send aid through the front door of Gaza. Meanwhile Palestinians have been forced to play a very real and deadly game of The Floor Is Lava when trying to access supplies, frequently finding themselves targeted by snipers while trying to obtain food and water.

•

There's a motherfucking genocide happening and we're being told we need to be worried about TikTok and defaced portraits of Lord Balfour.

•

Empire managers really seem to believe they can ban TikTok and kids will go "Oh well I guess I'll start reading The Atlantic and supporting genocide then."

•

Progressive Democrats who try to tell you that it's important to support Biden even though he's committing a genocide because he might do some nice things for Americans domestically are actually giving you a useful insight into exactly what's so evil about western liberalism.

•

Day after day after day we learn about new unbelievably fucked up things Israel is doing, but every time anyone responds to this deluge of information with a "Wow Israel's pretty fucked up, hey?" they get people yelling "Oh so I guess you have a problem with JEWS! Okay, Hitler."

And what's funny is this really, truly isn't about Jews. Both Zionists and genuine antisemites try to make such criticisms about Judaism and Jewishness, but that's just baby-brained analysis. You could take pretty much any ethnic or religious makeup and replace them with the ones at play in Israel-Palestine dynamics and you'd see the same types of abuses. You'd see that state requiring nonstop war, violence, apartheid and abuse in order to maintain its status quo, and you'd routinely see footage of members of the supremacist group behaving like monsters toward the victim group.

Did you know studies have shown that being wealthy reduces a person's empathy? Just that one tiered social system placing the wealthy above the non-wealthy turns the elevated class into garbage human beings. How much worse can we expect the privileged group to be in an ethno-supremacist apartheid state, where members of the privileged group are indoctrinated from birth into believing all kinds of justifications for this abusive dynamic?

There is literally no criticism you could possibly level at Israel that would not get you accused of antisemitism if you said it to a large enough audience, but this isn't about Jews, it's about abuse and injustice. The majority of the most moral and upstanding people I follow for ideas and information about the world happen to be Jewish; Jews are some of the best people I know. You either support an abusive apartheid ethnostate which can't exist without being in a constant state of war or you don't, and the majority of the people who do are not even Jewish. Anti-semitism is just an accusation that shitty people level at good people to divert criticisms of their shitty position.

Featured image via Adobe Stock.

A picture showing aid drops and Israeli airstrikes targeting civilian areas in northern Gaza at the same time.

This Is What Our Ruling Class Has Decided Will Be Normal

US airman Aaron Bushnell said the words "This is what our ruling class has decided will be normal" before self-immolating in protest of the genocide in Gaza. That simple line has been reverberating throughout our collective consciousness ever since.

It seems like every day now we're learning some horrible new fact about the US-centralized power alliance and the empire managers who carry out its malignant will for our world, because that's just what our rulers have decided will be the norm for our species going forward.

Reports that Israel tortured UN workers to extract false testimony against Gaza's primary humanitarian aid agency.

Images surfacing of airstrikes on Gaza occurring at the same time and location as airdrops of aid.

Gazan children beginning to drop dead from hunger in a deliberately-engineered famine that is causing sweeping starvation at breakneck speed.

The IDF kettling the population of Gaza further and further south with a horrifically destructive onslaught and then setting up an attack on the enclave's densely-packed southernmost point.

Israeli "demonstrators" bringing cotton candy machines and bouncy castles to create a fun, family-friendly atmosphere for their blockades to stop aid trucks from getting into Gaza.

The US president waxing poetically about how "heartbreaking" all the death and destruction in Gaza is when he himself is directly responsible for that death and destruction.

People in the world's most powerful nation being told they have to choose between two candidates who both support this genocide.

A journalist locked away in a maximum-security prison for factual reporting on the same empire which claims to support free speech and a free press.

The biosphere we depend on for survival being fed into a soulless profit-generating death machine because everything on our planet has been turned into a commodity.

The leaders of nuclear-armed states brandishing armageddon weapons at each other because a few manipulators in Washington DC and Virginia have decided that the US must maintain global hegemony at all cost.

A mind-controlled dystopia in which ordinary people are propagandized into accepting all this as perfectly fine.

This is what our ruling class has decided will be normal.

This madness will continue until we come together and resolutely decide the opposite.

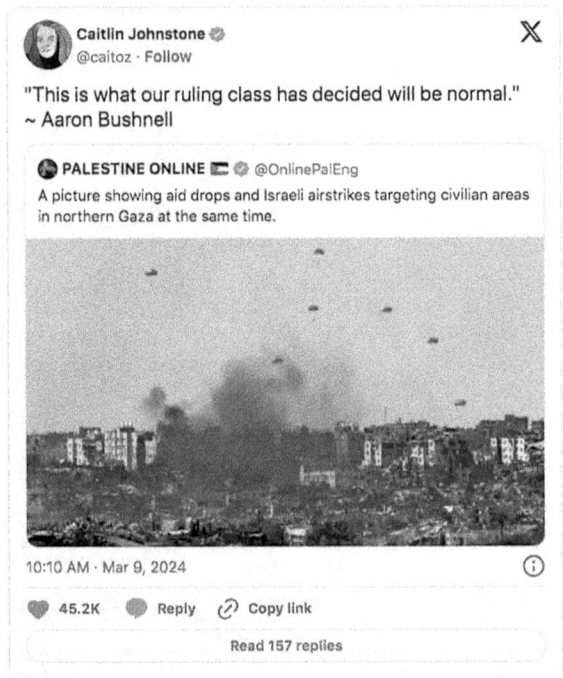

Caitlin Johnstone ✔
@caitoz · Follow

"This is what our ruling class has decided will be normal."
~ Aaron Bushnell

PALESTINE ONLINE ✔ @OnlinePalEng
A picture showing aid drops and Israeli airstrikes targeting civilian areas in northern Gaza at the same time.

10:10 AM · Mar 9, 2024

45.2K   Reply   Copy link

Read 157 replies

·

Naftali Bennett נפתלי בנט ✓
@naftalibennett

Fmr Prime Minister Naftali Bennett:

Regardless of our political opinion, we strongly oppose external political intervention in Israel's internal affairs.

We are an independent nation, not a banana republic.

With the threat of terrorism on its way to the West, it would be best if the international community would assist Israel in its just war, thereby also protecting their countries.

3:07 AM · Mar 15, 2024 · **1.1M** Views

If Israel Wants To Be An "Independent Nation", Let It Be An Independent Nation

In a continuation of the Democratic Party's weird new tactic of trying to assign Benjamin Netanyahu all the blame for the PR crisis caused by Israel's genocidal atrocities in Gaza, Senate Majority Leader Chuck Schumer denounced the Israeli prime minister on Thursday and called for new elections in Israel.

"As a lifelong supporter of Israel, it has become clear to me: The Netanyahu coalition no longer fits the needs of Israel after October 7. The world has changed, radically, since then, and the Israeli people are being stifled right now by a governing vision that is stuck in the past," said Schumer, adding, "At this critical juncture, I believe a new election is the only way to allow for a healthy and open decision-making process about the future of Israel, at a time when so many Israelis have lost their confidence in the vision and direction of their government."

Netanyahu's Likud party responded with an indignant statement saying that Schumer is "expected to respect Israel's elected government and not undermine it."

"Israel is not a banana republic, but an independent and proud democracy that elected Prime Minister Netanyahu," the statement said.

"Regardless of our political opinion, we strongly oppose external political intervention in Israel's internal affairs. We are an independent nation, not a banana republic," echoed former Israeli prime minister Naftali Bennett.

"With the threat of terrorism on its way to the West, it would be best if the international community would assist Israel in its just war, thereby also protecting their countries," Bennett added, an assertion that is ridiculous in multiple ways. There's no basis for the claim that the threat of terrorism is growing in the west, there is no basis for the claim that Israel's genocide in Gaza is a "just war", and there is no basis for the suggestion that helping Israel kill Palestinians in Gaza makes the western world safer in any way.

The Israeli right wing's repeated use of the term "banana republic" is both pointed and revealing. The term was coined in 1904 by O Henry to describe the Central American states which US imperialists ruled with an iron fist in order to exploit their people's labor at robbery prices for the immensely profitable export of tropical fruit. The insinuation being that it's fine when the US dictates the governmental affairs of the brown-skinned people south of its own border, but it's unacceptable for the US to do this to Israel.

We saw this point driven home in even starker terms with a Council on Foreign Relations piece titled "Schumer's Attack on an Ally at War" by virulent neocon Elliott Abrams. Abrams calls Schumer's mild finger-wagging "an unconscionable interference in the internal politics of another democracy", claiming the American senator is trying to treat Israel like a "colony" of the United States by controlling its internal affairs. Which is hilarious, given that just a few years ago Abrams was openly working to stage a coup in Venezuela under the Trump administration.

More to the point though, we should probably pay attention to this absurd claim that Israel is an "independent" nation.

Calling Israel an independent nation is like calling a fetus in the womb an independent person. It's like looking at a man in a hospital bed whose body is full of tubes and medical devices who needs to be manually repositioned every two hours to prevent him from getting pressure sores, and calling him independent.

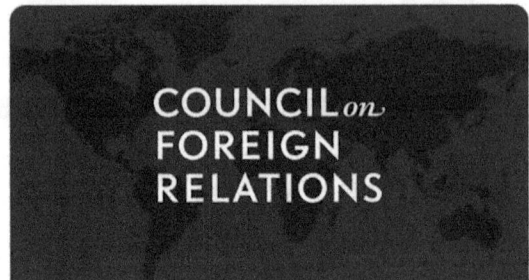

Israel is as dependent as a nation can possibly be. It literally cannot exist without the direct military backing of the most powerful empire of all time, namely the United States and its globe-spanning network of allies and assets.

Last November a retired Israeli major general named Yitzhak Brick told a columnist with the Jewish News Syndicate, "All of our missiles, the ammunition, the precision-guided bombs, all the airplanes and bombs, it's all from the US. The minute they turn off the tap, you can't keep fighting. You have no capability... Everyone understands that we can't fight this war without the United States. Period."

That is not how one talks about an "independent nation".

Israel knows it's fully dependent on the US empire, which is why it pours so much energy into lobbying in the US and its imperial member states like the UK. Israel cannot exist without nonstop violence, and it cannot sustain that nonstop violence without the backing of the US imperial war machine.

The reason Israel cannot exist without nonstop violence is because it is an artificial nation that was simply dropped on top of a pre-existing civilization whose inhabitants and neighbors had a deeply-rooted way of living which was massively disrupted by the sudden imposition of a newly created ethnostate ruled by people who'd never lived there before. Its emergence was so forced and unnatural that Zionists literally revived a dead middle eastern language called Hebrew and made it their national language so they could LARP as indigenous people speaking in their native tongue.

Because this alien synthetic ethnostate was abruptly forced upon an ancient pre-existing civilization with no regard for the humanity of the people living there, ever since this occurred the region's indigenous populations have been rejecting it like a body rejecting an ill-matched organ. The only way for the state of Israel to remain the state of Israel is therefore to exist in a continuous state of war, like a house that can only remain standing if it's got a giant team of construction workers toiling in perpetuity to stop it from falling over.

But if Israeli right-wingers wants to pretend none of this is happening, that's fine. Let Israel be an "independent nation" if that's what they want. Stop sending it arms, stop being its ally, stop bombing Yemen, Iraq and Syria in facilitation of its current military onslaught, stop providing it with intelligence, training and logistics support, stop operating in tandem with its military and intelligence services in the region, stop allowing its lobbyists and influence campaigns to operate in the United States, and stop providing its atrocities with diplomatic cover and mass media narrative spin. See how long Israel can stand independently if that occurs.

Of course, it won't happen. The managers of the US empire know their agendas of global hegemony benefit greatly from having a fully dependent and intimate ally in a region as geostrategically crucial as the middle east (which is why they allow the Israel lobby to continue to exist), and Israel knows it isn't actually independent in any meaningful sense of the word. But the fact that the US and Israel are so inextricable shows what a joke it is to pretend that this is a normal nation independently going about its own affairs like any other.

•

Podcast And Videos

Just letting our readers know that we now have both a podcast, and high quality videos.

We've managed to get three podcast episodes up! Recording it and making enough time to create it and edit it are skills we're still developing, but we've always learned on the job in this weird little project of ours anyway.

We've been answering reader questions such as:

"Discuss the reasons explaining the impressive level of US support for Israel."

"How do you maintain such productivity in the face of the negativity you're dealing with daily? Mindset, routines, practices?"

"Why weren't you so ragey about the civil war waged on Syrians by Assad about a decade ago, where far more were slaughtered than in Gaza right now?"

"We talk about pro-war corporate media narratives all the time. Who is the narrator? How is the script passed down?"

"Why Joe Biden and Netanyahu are not Behind the Bars?"

You can listen on Substack (where you will also receive an email every time a new podcast goes up) as well as all the normal places like Apple Podcasts, Google Podcasts, Spotify, Soundcloud, etc.

We've also started making regular high-quality video versions of many of the articles in this magazine for anyone who prefers to take them in video format. They all have subtitles accompanying a reading of the article by my husband Tim, often with relevant screenshots and the occasional fun gag thrown in.

We try to share our work in as many media as I can to reach the broadest audience possible. I've posted a few videos below so you can see what they look like and if they're your cup of tea. If they are, you can subscribe to my YouTube channel and view my articles that way from here on out if you prefer. If not, the written versions will always be here too.

Liberals Are Always Trying To Distance Biden From Netanyahu, And Netanyahu From Israel

Western liberals are always doing this weird dance where they try to rhetorically create space between Biden and the atrocities of the Israeli government, working tirelessly to frame the president as an innocent passive witness to the genocide he is directly facilitating in Gaza. Those western liberals who support Israel are also simultaneously performing a second bizarre contortion in which they try to distance the Israeli state from Benjamin Netanyahu, as though Israel would be a nice, normal, non-genocidal nation if it only had a different prime minister.

Biden breaks with Netanyahu but sticks with Israel

Barak Ravid

Two good examples of this frantic compartmentalization campaign came out in the mass media in the last few days, with a New York Times article titled "Providing Both Bombs and Food, Biden Puts Himself in the Middle of Gaza's War" and an Axios article titled "Biden breaks with Netanyahu but sticks with Israel".

Both the New York Times and Axios write-ups go out of their way to inform the reader that Biden has been growing "frustrated" with the Netanyahu government—yet more examples of a trend in liberal media reporting that's been going on for months in which spinmeisters convey the idea that Biden is secretly hopping mad at Bibi and his cohorts behind the scenes despite all of his actions and decisions and public statements conveying the opposite. The idea is to manipulate the reader into accepting that while Biden may be backing a genocide, secretly his feelings feel very upset at the people he's backing so you should like him and vote for him anyway.

The New York Times' Peter Baker and Michael Crowley present a poetical reframing of Biden's genocide in which they depict this lifelong Beltway swamp monster's self-evident depravity as a poignant story about a kindhearted leader facing difficult decisions, saying "The United States finds itself on both sides of the war in a way, arming the Israelis while trying to care for those hurt as a result."

"From the skies over Gaza these days fall American bombs and American food pallets, delivering death and life at the same time and illustrating President Biden's elusive effort to find balance in an unbalanced Middle East war," write Baker and Crowley, presumably while high-fiving about their eloquent prose.

"Mr. Biden has grown increasingly frustrated as Prime Minister Benjamin Netanyahu of Israel defies the president's pleas to do more to protect civilians in Gaza and went further in expressing that exasperation during and after his State of the Union address this past week," write the authors, before adding, "But Mr. Biden remains opposed to cutting off munitions or leveraging them to influence the fighting."

That last sentence right there is all anyone needs to know about Joseph R Biden. Those are the raw facts, and everything else is narrative spin. Israel gets the actual material weapons it requires to continue its

Nathan J Robinson
@NathanJRobinson · Follow

according the Israel Democracy Institute, 2/3 of Jewish Israelis support starving Gazan children to death
en.idi.org.il/articles/52976

> provision of international aid to the residents o
> for their opinion regarding the idea that Israel s
> humanitarian aid to Gaza residents at this tim
> linked to Hamas or to UNRWA. A majority of J
> transfer of humanitarian aid even under these
> Arab respondents support it (85%).

3:26 AM · Mar 12, 2024

290   Reply   Copy link

Read 16 replies

genocidal atrocities, and the readers of The New York Times get empty narrative fluff about aid drops and Biden's feelings to help them feel okay about it.

Axios' Barak Ravid is somehow even more ham-fisted, writing that "President Biden has begun a tricky maneuver: breaking with Israeli Prime Minister Benjamin Netanyahu and his Gaza war strategy—while sticking with Israel and its fight against Hamas."

"U.S. officials say Biden—and many other senior officials at the White House and the State Department—are extremely frustrated by what they see as ungratefulness by Netanyahu," writes Ravid, because when you're writing about Biden and Gaza in a liberal publication you're required to work that "frustrated" angle in somewhere.

To substantiate his claim that Biden is "breaking" with Netanyahu, Ravid references Biden's oblique finger-wagging at "the leadership of Israel" in his State of the Union address and the president's "I told Bibi 'You and I are going to have a come-to-Jesus meeting'" hot mic moment immediately thereafter, as well as Biden's statement on MSNBC that Netanyahu is "hurting Israel more than helping Israel" by tarnishing Israel's image.

Then, immediately thereafter, Ravid nullifies everything he just wrote in the preceding paragraphs by noting another quote from Biden's MSNBC appearance: "I'm never gonna leave Israel. The defense of Israel is still critical."

Liberals love pretending there's a meaningful difference between supporting Netanyahu's murderousness and supporting Israel, as though Israeli murderousness does not have a healthy and vibrant existence entirely independent of who its prime minister happens to be. Pinning all the blame for Israel's depravity on one evil bad guy lets them justify their continued support for Israel despite that position's self-evident contradiction with everything they claim to stand for.

Polling by the Israel Democracy Institute has found that three-quarters of Jewish Israelis support Netanyahu's planned assault on Rafah, which the prime minister has said will proceed as planned despite Biden's empty bloviations that doing so would be crossing a "red line" with this administration. Polls also found that 68 percent of Jewish Israelis oppose any humanitarian aid entering Gaza via any agency at all, which is to say they support starving huge numbers of Gazan civilians to death.

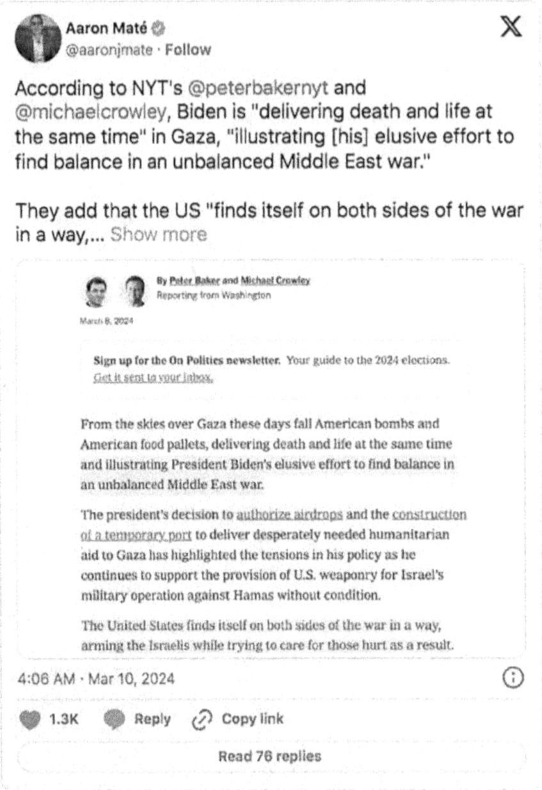

Aaron Maté
@aaronjmate · Follow

According to NYT's @peterbakernyt and @michaelcrowley, Biden is "delivering death and life at the same time" in Gaza, "illustrating [his] elusive effort to find balance in an unbalanced Middle East war."

They add that the US "finds itself on both sides of the war in a way,... Show more

By Peter Baker and Michael Crowley
Reporting from Washington

March 8, 2024

Sign up for the On Politics newsletter. Your guide to the 2024 elections. Get it sent to your inbox.

From the skies over Gaza these days fall American bombs and American food pallets, delivering death and life at the same time and illustrating President Biden's elusive effort to find balance in an unbalanced Middle East war.

The president's decision to authorize airdrops and the construction of a temporary port to deliver desperately needed humanitarian aid to Gaza has highlighted the tensions in his policy as he continues to support the provision of U.S. weaponry for Israel's military operation against Hamas without condition.

The United States finds itself on both sides of the war in a way, arming the Israelis while trying to care for those hurt as a result.

4:06 AM · Mar 10, 2024

1.3K Reply Copy link

Read 76 replies

Israeli violence isn't the product of Netanyahu, Netanyahu is the product of Israeli violence. He built his political career upon popular sentiments that were already in place long before he turned up. If it wasn't him inflicting violence and abuse on Palestinians it would be someone else, and it has been in the past, and it will continue to be for as long as Israel exists.

There is no state of Israel that is separate or separable from the violence, abuse, apartheid and racist indoctrination necessary for its continued existence. Liberals like to pretend they live in this imaginary fantasyland where a nice and peaceful Israel is possible, despite Israel's entire historical existence making an obvious lie of this premise.

Israeli violence is not distant from Israel; they are fully united. Israel is not distant from Netanyahu; they are not meaningfully distinct. Netanyahu is not distant from Biden; they are partners in every way that matters. Liberals only try to compartmentalize these things away from each other to stave off the cognitive dissonance inherent in their contradiction-soaked worldview.

•

I Don't Need Guns I Need Fire Extinguishers

Pointing pistols as the man burns,
as Gaza burns,
as civilization burns,
as the planet burns.
I don't need guns
I need fire extinguishers.

Raytheon racketeers and Pentagon pimps
swollen fat from the blood of unnamed victims
glossed over in headlines by The New York Times
while National Guard troops patrol the New York subways
and babies with legs like toothpicks fill our screens.
Pouring arms into Israel
while humanitarian-LARPing aid airdrops.
Waving around armageddon weapons
while accusing peacemongers of treason.
Well sure I'd ask for seconds mister president sir,
but see I don't need guns
I need fire extinguishers.

I need someone to put some fat back on those babies.
I need someone to get the plastic out of the oceans.
I need the bombs to stop and the siege to lift
and a healthy planet for the kids to play in.
I need kids to stop getting their limbs blown off
so they can run and play in that healthy world.
Can you drone strike me a thriving biosphere?
Can you ICBM those Gazans some food?
Can you extinguish this fire with your weapons and wars?
No?
Then get outta the way man.
We don't need guns
we need fire extinguishers.

"Free Palestine," the man on fire said.
"FREE PALESTINE!" he screamed.
And then the cops showed up with their guns and their bullets,
because of course they fucking did.
And Gaza still burns,
and the world still burns,
and our eyes still burn,
and our lungs still burn,
and our hearts still burn,
and our rage still burns,
and they promise us the burning will stop
if we just add in a few more guns.

We don't need guns you stupid cop.
We need this burning world to heal.

•

https://www.caitlinjohnst.one

JOHNSTONE is a completely reader-funded project by Caitlin Johnstone and Tim Foley. To find out how you can support us, visit: caitlinjohnstone.com.au/about/

Coverart by Caitlin Johnstone featuring an original oil painting by Caitlin Johnstone
"The Self-Immolation Of Aaron Bushnell", oil on canvas, 30" x 20"